TENACITY

Hoot on the Appalachian Trail

Gregory F. West
with **Stephanie F. West**

Published by **Elevation Publishing Group, LLC.**
Cover design by **DeVasha Lloyd**

Hardback ISBN: 979-8-9999460-3-4
Paperback ISBN: 979-8-9999460-4-1
eBook ISBN: 979-8-9999460-5-8

Printed in United States of America

For more information, visit:

www.elevationpublishing.com

(Page intentionally left blank)

Prologue

Greg

I've always called 2008 my roller-coaster year.

It started on a high note when my son Jarrod married Colleen, a brilliant, kind woman we instantly loved. But that joy was short-lived. In April, my father-in-law took a terrible fall and ended up in the hospital. We were all worried, especially my wife Peggy.

Then came September, and we celebrated again when our daughter Larissa married the love of her life, also named Gregg with 2 "g's", so the family called him "Greggggg" to differentiate him from me!

But just two months later, in November, everything changed. Peggy died suddenly. She was only 57. The holidays after her passing were a blur. My four kids and I did our best to hold each other up, but nothing felt the same. I looked at the pictures from that time later and barely recognized myself—gray, hollow-eyed, trying to smile for their sake.

And fate wasn't done. In February 2009, I lost my job during the recession. After more than 30 years with one company, I was laid off. My salary had become too big a target during the economic downturn.

A devout Roman Catholic, I recall shaking my fist at the heavens and crying out, "What else can you do to me?"

~~~

Oddly enough, losing that job brought something I hadn't had in decades: freedom. With Sarah, my youngest, and her toddler still living at home, I wasn't alone entirely. But without a boss or a commute, I had time to breathe. I rode my bike. I took long walks when the Buffalo, NY weather allowed. I spent hours in the woodshop. I babysat my grandson.

Still, after 34 years of marriage, I felt the ache of loss every day. I wasn't just unemployed. I was a widower. And I was lonely.

Stephanie

Stephanie moved into the neighborhood in 2006, ready for a fresh chapter after the end of a long-term relationship. Her son, Bryan, had just finished his first year in the Navy, but he took a short leave to help her move. He gathered a few of his high school friends and made sure his mom and her three cats were settled into her new home.

It was the first time Stephanie had ever lived alone. She had always shared space with a roommate, a partner, or her son. Bryan gave her a playful look as he surveyed the scene and said, "Now don't you become the neighborhood crazy cat lady, Mom." He said it with a grin, but knowing she had moved to Buffalo years earlier to work in a feline-only veterinary clinic, he had reason to worry that cats might once again become the center of her world.

But life kept Stephanie busy. She juggled a couple of veterinary jobs and filled her free time with volunteer work. Her cats only saw her in the evenings, when she came home to rest. Soon after moving in, as her new neighbor, I had left a kind, handwritten note with Peggy's and my names, our phone number, and a warm invitation: *"Stop by anytime."* Stephanie appreciated the gesture, but she never did stop by. Occasionally, she'd wave from her yard when she saw us over the chain-link fence, and that was the extent of it.

Then one evening in late 2008, everything shifted.

A neighbor knocked on her door to share the devastating news that Peggy had collapsed suddenly and was in the hospital. It didn't look good. Two days later, after a long drive, Stephanie pulled into her driveway late at night and noticed me pacing the sidewalk, looking lost.

For the first time since she'd moved in, she walked over and gently asked how I was doing.

I don't remember much of what I said that night, but Stephanie does. She remembers I opened up, grieving, heartbroken, still reeling from the loss of my wife earlier that day. She listened quietly, offering nothing more than her presence and a kind word or two.

We parted ways soon after. Neither of us could have known at that moment how much that quiet conversation would come to mean.

A Beginning

In the spring of 2009, I decided to try dating again.

At the age of 57, I had almost no dating experience because I was fortunate to have married my late wife Peggy right after graduating from Buffalo State College. I remember how proud I was to attend college because I was the first in my blue-collar family to reach that milestone. But it felt like stepping into completely unknown territory.

Peggy and I met at a local nightclub, both there to see an up-and-coming musician named Bob Seger. Her long blonde hair first caught my eye, then her blue eyes captured me when I asked her to dance. She admired my green bellbottoms with a classy white pinstripe. She was a nursing student at a nearby hospital, not far from my college. We started dating right away and married once we had both graduated. We had been married just short of 35 years when I lost her.

Half a year after Peggy passed away, I signed up for an online dating site and went on a few dates. Mostly, I was looking for company and trying to stay open to whatever might happen, but my kids were worried I was trying to replace their mom.

I tried, in vain, to explain to them that I missed their mom terribly and that no one could ever replace her. It was the loneliness that was hard. In response, they told my youngest daughter, Sarah, to stay in the house with her son and "keep an eye on Dad," to make sure I wasn't alone too much. They'd had their own run-ins with the modern dating world and worried that their loving, generous, and, in their words, "naïve" father was bound to get hurt.

Then, on June 23, 2009, I was browsing in the local bookstore when I looked up and saw my neighbor, Stephanie, standing nearby, engrossed in a book. I couldn't resist. With my usual quirky sense of humor, I leaned in and whispered in her ear, "They let anyone in here, don't they?"

She jumped a little and then laughed when she saw it was me.

We started talking, and she told me she was there on the advice of a friend who'd been pushing her to "journal her heart," stop being such a workaholic, and maybe start dating again. I told her I was trying to date again, too. Then, feeling uncharacteristically bold, I asked, "Well, when are we going to go on a date?"

She just pointed over to the coffee shop in the store and said, "How about now?"

We sat and talked for three hours. The next night, we met again for a walk, and before I knew it, we were talking and connecting every single day. I didn't even notice when my online dating subscription expired.

We talked endlessly, trying to fill in the decades of life we hadn't shared, and the more we talked, the more comfortable we were with each other. At one point, Stephanie asked me what my dreams and desires were. I told her, honestly, that I didn't have time for dreams. She pushed me, wouldn't let it go, and finally, half-joking and half-serious, I told her I hadn't had a real dream since I was 25, when I wanted to hike the Appalachian Trail.

And that was the beginning of everything.

Table of Contents

Chapter 1

It Begins

Georgia

March 7, 2012 – Wednesday

Spring was whispering its arrival in northern Georgia, the green just beginning to tease the edges of brown. The sun hinted at warmth, but the air still had a bite to it that reminded us winter hadn't fully released its grip.

We pulled into the parking lot at Amicalola Falls State Park, and when the engine shut off, a hush fell over all of us.

"Are we really going to do this?" My nephew Michael asked, half in awe, half in panic.

I laughed, and just like that, we opened the doors and stepped out, two hikers and our support team. Stephanie and my sister Pam followed as we made our way to the Visitor's Center.

Outside, a hook and scale hung from a roof beam, an invitation for hikers starting the Appalachian Trail to weigh their packs. I lifted my pack and felt its weight settle onto my shoulders. Forty-seven pounds. Michael's was forty-one. Between us, we'd split the load of tent, stove, food, and all the essentials for surviving the next six months.

This trip had been a dream of mine for years, one I'd never thought I would really attempt. But last summer, when Stephanie first met Pam, she mentioned my dream to my sister and said how I'd always wanted to hike the AT but wasn't sure I should go solo. Without missing a beat, Pam offered up her son. She said he loved the woods and wanted to hike the AT someday anyway. She'd feel better if her brother and her son went together.

Stephanie and Pam had spent the six months since then quietly worrying and actively planning. They gathered maps, gear, food drops, and packing strategies. This moment wasn't just the beginning of my journey; it was theirs, too.

That morning, Pam drove all four of us three hours from Knoxville, TN, where we'd done the final prep. At the Visitor's Center, Michael and I bypassed the museum displays and wildlife warnings. Our focus was on the logbook. We stepped up to the counter and signed our names as hikers #198 and #199 for 2012.

Declaring yourself a thru-hiker in that logbook isn't legally binding, but in your heart, it's a contract. Fewer than a quarter of those who start the trail finish it in one season. But we weren't thinking of that. We were thinking: *We're doing this.*

We walked through the stone archway at 10:30 a.m., crunching over dry leaves on the Approach Trail. Stephanie and Pam stood behind, watching us go, holding back emotion as they snapped a few last pictures.

I didn't turn around. Not because I wasn't thinking of them, but because I was carrying them with me. In every carefully packed meal, in the hugs they'd given as we left them behind, and in every bit of faith they had placed in us.

That first step was more than just the start of a hike. It was a shared leap of trust. And it had finally begun.

It didn't take long for me to realize Michael was much faster than me. That wasn't a surprise, really. I turned 60 last October, and my knees weren't exactly thrilled about the idea of hiking nearly 2,200 miles. They let me know that loud and clear the moment we hit the trail.

I trained all winter in Buffalo, NY by trudging up and down snow-covered bleachers at a nearby school with a full pack, and walking every day that the weather allowed, but nothing really prepares you for the Appalachian Trail. The actual AT was much more difficult than my Buffalo training hikes, with uneven terrain and constant elevation changes.

We started with the Approach Trail, which is 8.8 miles just to get to the *start* of the Appalachian Trail. It began with 425 stairs running straight up alongside a waterfall. By the time we reached the top of Springer Mountain five hours later, we were sweaty, sore, and wondering what we'd gotten ourselves into.

We flopped onto the summit's wide, flat rock, sprawled like beached whales, and took the obligatory photo next to the bronze plaque marking the AT's southern terminus. That's when we noticed the other hikers. Relaxed, chipper, barely winded. Turns out you can bypass the entire Approach Trail and get dropped off near the summit by car.

We looked at each other, sweaty, aching, and just laughed. We hiked 8.8 miles and hadn't even *started* the official trail yet.

While Michael and I were finding our trail legs, Stephanie and Pam were navigating a different kind of wilderness, Georgia backroads with no cell signal. After dropping us off, they wound their way through the hills until they reached a hiker hostel near Hiawassee. That's where they dropped off our first food box: carefully pre-packed ziplocks with everything we'd need to eat for the next stretch. We were carrying only four days of food, because we knew we could purchase a few more days of food at the first little hamlet of Neel's Gap, but then we'd be too far from civilization to find a food store. We had carefully planned our hike and the necessary food drops we'd need. Hiawassee was the first of these. Little did we know that an AT hike shredded plans.

Breakfast bags had oatmeal, dried fruit, instant coffee, or tea. Lunch was variations of GORP, "Good Ole Raisins and Peanuts" (otherwise known as trail mix) or energy bars.

Dinners were packaged meat, a spice or sauce packet, and dried rice or noodles. Outer packaging was removed to decrease weight and trash to be carried out. Each day of food adds about two pounds to the pack weight, so 5-7 days was generally the most food a hiker carried. We would carry just enough of the ziplock bags for the planned number of days to the next food drop.

The food they dropped off at our first planned pick-up stop was sealed in a box labeled "Hold for Northbound AT Hikers," with the hiker names and anticipated date that we were expected to be at that shelter, in about a week. (Carrying more than a week's worth of food made the pack too heavy, which is why we had these food drops and resupply plans, spaced out like breadcrumbs all the way to Maine.)

After dropping off the food package, Pam and Stephanie stopped at a local fast-food joint to stress-eat junk food. They had maintained their good cheer and positivity to send off their hikers, but now confessed to each other how anxious they were about the entire adventure.

Relieved to discover that each felt similarly, they piled back in the white SUV and returned to Knoxville, TN. From there, Stephanie drove back to Buffalo, NY, and both returned to their "normal" lives, with Pam on-call for emergencies if needed, while we hikers traversed the first few southern states.

Planning for food, maps, and gear replenishment was an important prerequisite to the hike. While there are roads that cross the AT, getting to a food store often requires a long hike or a hitched ride off the trail. This adds time and effort to the AT hike, and most hikers carefully calculate where and how to resupply. Having a helper, or "Trail Angel" back home is very useful. Pam and Stephanie were the Trail Angels for Michael and me. The hike of almost 2,200 miles had a definite end date; October 15 or the first snowfall on the northern terminus of the AT, at Mount Katahdin in Maine, whichever came first. With the snowfall or the October 15th date, Baxter State Park around Mount Katahdin closes with no exceptions allowed, leaving hikers to wait for the next year to summit Mount Katahdin and complete the AT. Since snow often came earlier to northern Maine, I was hoping to complete the adventure by September, for a total of six months on the AT.

That would require an average hike of about 12 miles per day with no stops. Realistically, hikers do take rest and relaxation days, also called "Zero" days, where they rest and cover no miles. This is crucial for their health and well-being but also must be calculated into the plan of a thru-hiker. Resting for too many days may lead to the fearful plight of northbound AT hikers who intended to complete the entire hike in one season being turned back in sight of the end by the closing of Baxter State Park. Any days lost as a Zero meant mileage to be made up on hiking days. Therefore, the calculation of mileage and overall pace was almost an obsession with the thru-hiker crowd.

After a rest and a quick text to Pam and Stephanie with the picture of us by the Springer Mountain plaque as proof of starting the official AT, we pushed on an additional 2.8 miles to get to the first shelter, Stover Creek.

The shelter was packed, but we found space in the loft. Around us, the culture of the AT began to reveal itself: hikers had already adopted "trail names," quirky monikers taken on like badges. There were Blue, Phoenix, Maine-iac. And August, an experienced hiker who held court by a blazing fire, sharing stories and charming everyone within earshot.

I wasn't quite ready to be part of that world yet. I went off into the woods with Michael to cook our first dinner, and it was a disaster. The little stove didn't heat evenly, and our packaged meal turned into a lukewarm blend of chewy rice and gritty sauce. We ate in silence under the trees, wondering if we were cut out for this.

That night, I crawled into my sleeping bag exhausted, aching from head to toe. My hips hurt. My shoulders throbbed. My head was cold, so I pulled the bag up over my ears and tried to will myself to sleep.

I didn't sleep much. But I wasn't scared. Not yet. There was too much adrenaline. Too much wonder.

The trail had begun.

The next morning, we set out on our first full day of hiking the AT, **Thursday, March 8th**. After an 8 a.m. wake-up and a breakfast of packaged oatmeal (cooked through), we got underway about 8:40 a.m.

We climbed up to Hawk Mountain shelter (elevation about 3400 feet) by about 11:00 a.m., not even 6 miles. Some of the hikers chose to stop there for the day, for an easier pace, but Michael and I decided to push on to the next shelter, about 7 miles further.

After the initial climb, it was fairly flat. However, there are always some ups and downs as most of the hills and mountains are separated by deep valleys, or gaps. My breathing was rough on the uphills, and the downhills pounded my arthritic knees. This was much, much harder than I anticipated! There wasn't even scenery to enjoy, as the day was cold, misty and foggy. The trees were still winter bare, except for the intermittent white paint blazes that marked the trail, and the trail wound through monotonous leaf litter and rocks.

Michael pushed on at his faster pace. I put my head down to avoid the rain and plodded along the quiet trail.

Sometime in the afternoon, I finally reached a stretch of trail that leveled out, a gift after so many miles of endless climbing and careful footing. I paused to catch my breath and looked up, only to nearly stop breathing altogether.

There, in the misty quiet of the woods, was a machine gun aimed squarely at me. My heart jumped. I turned my head slightly and spotted camouflaged soldiers. They stood silent and completely still, like part of the forest itself.

I did what any overly polite, stunned man with sore knees and a heavy pack might do, I nodded at them. Respectfully. Casually. Like we were just two groups of folks out for a walk in the same patch of woods. They didn't move, didn't say a word. Just watched.

Soon, I crossed a dirt road and passed military vehicles, people moving about with purpose. They didn't acknowledge me either, just let me pass through like I was invisible. I later learned it was likely part of a training exercise near a Ranger camp. The Rangers, apparently, are well known for giving AT hikers the right of way.

Still. It's not every day you walk through a live military training zone with no warning. One more surreal moment on a trail that was already blurring the line between reality and dream.

I made it to Gooch Mountain Shelter just before 5 p.m. after logging 13 miles and eight hours of steady hiking. Michael had already arrived. We found the shelter was full, so we pitched the two-man tent off to the side. Michael offered to cook that night, and I gladly handed over the stove. The meal was better than last night's half-crunchy rice disaster, but still nothing to write home about.

And honestly, even a gourmet dinner couldn't have fixed how I felt. I was discouraged. Everything hurt. My back, knees, hips. The kind of ache that seeps deep into your bones and settles in like an unwanted guest. It had started raining just as we zipped the tent shut, and now we were sealed inside, all damp, tired, and trapped in a nylon cocoon not quite big enough for comfort. Worst of all, I missed Stephanie.

We'd been together two and a half years, and somehow it wasn't the trail, or the pain, or the rain that got to me, it was missing her. Her laugh, her optimism, her way of making everything feel manageable, even when it wasn't.

I lay awake listening to the steady rhythm of rain tapping on the tent, wondering what on earth I'd signed myself up for. If there had been a way to leave the trail right then, I might have taken it. No shame, just honesty.

But that's the thing about the Appalachian Trail, it doesn't offer shortcuts. The only way out is forward. If I wanted off the trail, I'd have to walk my way out of it.

And if I was going to walk anyway … Well, I might as well keep going north.

With that thought, I finally drifted into a restless, damp sleep, rain still whispering across the tent above me like a lullaby for the tired and unsure.

Michael and I survived one full day on the trail. We awoke the next morning, **Friday, March 9th**, at 6:30 a.m. to discover that the rain had stopped. The tent had held up well in the downpour with only a minor leakage down at the base. But there was a casualty from the rain; my map and journal got wet.

Stephanie had purchased the complete set of AT maps from the Appalachian Trail Conservancy as a Christmas present for me. Each map covered the AT for a specific section, including useful information such as elevations, location of shelters, and any roads that the AT crossed. There were separate maps for various sections of the AT, so they didn't all have to be carried at once, and so the maps for new sections were also carefully planned to be sent forward along with the food drops as we hiked along the entire AT. The maps were on water-resistant paper, luckily, but it was annoying that my new journal got wet already. After that, I made sure to carefully place the small black journal in a ziplock bag from then on.

Everything was still wet in the morning, even though the rain had stopped. I had to pull on yesterday's cold, damp hiking clothes and pack away the one dry set I reserved for sleeping. Some hikers only carry a single outfit. Not me. I'd gladly take the extra weight for the luxury of something warm and dry to put on at the end of the day.

Still, there's nothing like sliding into soggy clothes first thing in the morning. It jolts your system, but the body heat builds up quickly once you start moving again. The first half hour on the trail is always cold and cranky—after that, your legs take over.

Before we left the shelter, I paid a visit to the composting privy—my first experience with one. Oddly efficient, even clean. I wouldn't see many like it until we got farther north. Most shelters along the AT have some kind of privy nearby, but when they don't … well, that's when the "cat hole" method comes into play. Some folks carry a trowel. Everyone carries their own toilet paper.

It's the little things that start to matter most.

We hiked a relatively short day, only 8 miles of rolling trail through forest and past Big Cedar Mountain, stopping just beyond Miller Gap at Lance Creek. It wasn't by chance. This was the last safe campsite before entering an area where bear canisters were required.

Apparently, there was a bear in that stretch who had figured out the classic "food bag in a tree" trick. The bear knew the woods better than we did—and had learned the hikers' routines. Rather than risk it, or carry the extra weight of a $70 canister, we planned to stay just shy of the boundary.

We made it to Lance Creek by early afternoon and pitched the tent in a soft, flat patch in the woods. It gave us time to dry out gear, dry out socks, dry out souls.

I tried calling Stephanie. No signal.

Before I left, we'd made this plan: a Friday "check-in" call each week. But the reality of the AT quickly taught us that signal is a gift, not a guarantee. Most shelters are nestled in low-lying gaps where cell service disappears completely. Eventually, we agreed I'd call or text whenever I had a signal, usually at the top of a mountain. Stephanie, ever the optimist, made a custom ringtone for my messages, so whenever I could reach her, she'd know right away.

That afternoon was still and quiet. No rain, no drama, just time. Time to breathe, to stretch, to feel our bodies rebel in new ways. My muscles ached. My feet throbbed. And that night, it got cold again—sharper than the previous night. We were still in the southern mountains, but elevation can be deceptive. Five degrees colder for every thousand feet. Some days, we climbed through multiple temperature zones without realizing it until we stopped moving.

I finally broke down and took ibuprofen, something I usually avoid. Even with it, I couldn't sleep well. Neither of us could. The ground was hard, and our minds were harder to quiet. I drifted into strange dreams, half-formed images of cities, faces, old memories. Nothing made sense. And when I woke up, it didn't feel like rest.

Still, it was another day behind us. Another day we didn't quit. And for now, that was enough.

The next day was **Saturday, March 10**, set to be our longest hike so far. Michael and I planned a long trek through the bear region to get to Neel's Gap.

This constitutes a store and hostel located at the first road after the start of the AT, a little over 30 miles from the beginning. Reportedly 20%-25% of the hikers that start the AT bail off the trail here after their first few days, having discovered that hiking the AT is uncomfortable and not for the faint of heart.

Michael and I pushed along the trail, climbing up and up, with rocks shoring up parts of the trail. After 5 miles of almost continual uphill climbing, I hoped we had reached the top of Blood Mountain. At 4500 feet, it is the tallest mountain on the Georgia section of the AT.

At the top of the next climb, Michael casually said, "This isn't Blood Mountain yet." My heart sank. I'd thought we were there.

But I had a signal, and I called Stephanie. I told her everything, the pain, the rain, how utterly hard this all was.

"This is much harder than I thought," I said. "Extremely difficult."

She didn't tell me to quit. She just listened and reminded me I could do hard things. Her voice gave me a shot of strength I desperately needed. We hiked down the mountain... and discovered that was Blood Mountain. The weight lifted instantly. I'd made it to Neel's Gap.

We reached the outfitter store just after noon and collapsed at the picnic area. I devoured a hot dog and gulped a sports drink—real food that didn't come out of a bag. I called Stephanie again, this time almost giddy. I needed her to hear my voice after that low call earlier.

We stocked up on food. It wasn't as expensive as we feared—another small win. Nearby, there was a pile of camping gear other hikers had abandoned. Someone from the store would go through your pack if you asked and rip out anything unnecessary. Michael and I congratulated ourselves on our efficient packing and laughed at some of the things people had carried 31.7 miles from Springer Mountain.

Then there were the boots. Dozens of them, hanging from the trees by their laces. A quiet tradition: if you quit the trail at Neel's Gap, you toss your boots. We saw all those boots and silently made a decision: we were *not* giving up. I had this fantasy of Stephanie pulling up in a car and whisking me away. But I also had this stubborn little flame inside me: *I hate it, but I won't let it beat me.*

We left Neel's Gap recharged. Michael was energized. The trail, however, was poorly marked. People imagine the AT as a nice gravel path. It's not.

It's a raw trek of rocks, roots, switchbacks, steep climbs, and it changes all the time. Floods, storms, erosion.

Every year the trail's total length shifts slightly. But finishing it earns you the title "2,000 Miler." That's what we were aiming for.

We stopped at our planned campsite, but the water source was barely a trickle. You can't hike without water. We pushed on to Bag's Creek Gap, where a small spring offered just enough. The next source was 3 miles away, and we were already at 12 for the day.

Two other hikers had already set up camp. Dave, a former Army Ranger from Pittsburgh, and Payton from Alabama. Dave explained the military training I'd unknowingly walked into earlier. We built a fire and shared trail stories around it. Everyone turned in by 7:30 p.m. It had been a long day.

Still, I couldn't sleep. That became the new norm. No matter how far I hiked, no matter how exhausted I was, the second I lay down, the pain caught up to me—and my mind wouldn't stop.

We started the next day, **Sunday March 11**, an hour late at 9 a.m. because it was Daylight Savings time.

I kept rigorous track of time to evaluate my hiking pace. This section of the trail was also poorly marked; not a lot of blazes, and the water supply was poor. Most of the day's walk was slightly uphill and on ridges. Michael and I had planned to only walk to Chattahoochee Gap, but ended up a little further at Blue Mountain Shelter with a lot of the same hikers we had seen along the way. The trek of over 14 miles meant that we just passed the 50-mile mark.

March 12, 2012 – Monday

We woke to a misty morning, the kind that muffles everything and makes the forest feel like a secret. The cool air wrapped around us as I packed up, eating my standard trail breakfast of oatmeal while Michael chewed on his usual fruit and nut bars. We hit the trail around 8:20 a.m., aiming for Tray Mountain Shelter. The mist slowly turned into rain, and visibility dropped to maybe 100 yards. Just as I was pulling on my rain gear, the fabric tore wide open. There I was—wet, cold, and utterly exposed to the elements.

We trudged over two 4,000-foot peaks in silence, the rain blurring everything around us. I couldn't see a view if I wanted to.

Hours passed like that—gray, wet, monotonous—and by the time we finally reached Tray Mountain Shelter, I was chilled to the bone.

I stripped off the soaked clothes and cooked up some hot soup with jerky, thinking we'd call it a day and hunker down there. It felt like a sensible decision.

But Michael had other ideas. He wanted to keep going.

It was the first time we really disagreed. My whole body protested the idea of walking even one more mile. Just then, a hiker we'd seen before— Brook, with his unmistakable red shoes—joined us. We later came to know him as "SpiceRack." He mentioned the rain was supposed to continue and might even turn into thunderstorms. He wisely chose to stay put. I hesitated... but in the end, I changed back into my wet clothes, gritted my teeth, and followed Michael back onto the trail.

We pushed on toward Deep Gap Shelter. It was a long, punishing walk. At some point, Michael tweaked his Achilles tendon, and the pain slowed him down significantly. I worried about him as we trudged forward, both of us utterly soaked and exhausted. By the time we stumbled into Deep Gap around 6:00 p.m., we had covered 15 rain-soaked miles.

The shelter was packed—15 or 16 wet, miserable hikers (and a dog) squeezed into a space meant for eight. One look was enough for us. We pitched the tent quickly during a brief lull in the downpour. I was too tired to cook, so we nibbled on cold food. The only small grace that night was that my second set of clothes was still dry. I slipped into them, climbed into my sleeping bag, and lay there listening to the rain hammering down, familiar now like an old enemy who won't leave.

March 13, 2012 – Tuesday

We woke to more rain, more fog, more wet gear. It felt never-ending. After a quick breakfast, we packed up and trudged the 3.5 miles to Dicks Creek Gap, where Michael's mom, Pam, would pick us up so Michael could tend to his Achille's heel injury. I hated the idea of taking a break, hated feeling like I was quitting. But as we sat waiting by the roadside, other hikers began to gather. Some injured, discouraged, just needing a breather. I realized we weren't the only ones feeling beat down. I wasn't alone. I wasn't failing. I was just human.

Fellow hikers Dave and Payton were also waiting for rides to take a rest. That made me feel a little less ashamed.

I later learned that Payton never came back. We'd pushed hard for seven days straight, and it had taken a toll.

Pam arrived and first drove us to Hiawasee to pick up the food drop that she and Stephanie had left for us. We wouldn't need it now. My legs ached, my back was a knot of pain, and yet the quiet ride with Pam felt like a turning point. I no longer saw the pause as weakness. I saw it as survival.

Later that Day – Knoxville, Tennessee

By 4:00 p.m., we were in Knoxville at Pam and Les's warm, welcoming home. The first hot shower in over a week was pure heaven. I called daughter Larissa and then Stephanie. Then I opened my email, and that's when it hit me.

Stephanie had collected dozens of encouraging messages from friends, family, and even former coworkers. I was floored. I hadn't known so many people were following our hike, let alone rooting for me. It brought tears to my eyes.

I had worked at the same company for over 30 years, first as a machinist, then as a CNC operator, and finally in a customer service role I hated. After being laid off in 2009 and re-hired at a reduced salary, I'd watched the job I once cared about become a source of daily dread. I came home each night more tired in spirit than in body. Stephanie saw it. She worried.

When my boss, Neil, suddenly died of a heart attack just before his planned retirement, it was a wake-up call. I asked for six months' unpaid leave to hike the AT. Management said no. That was the last straw.

"If you can't let me go to follow my dream after nearly 35 years," I told them, "then I can't keep working for you."

And I gave my two weeks' notice on the spot.

What I didn't realize was that my decision had a ripple effect. My coworkers—some of whom had been through decades of company changes, layoffs, and slow raises—saw me as proof that it was still possible to take back your life. They gave me small gifts and a card filled with messages. They even posted a giant map of the Appalachian Trail at work and followed my progress through Stephanie's updates. That card was the only non-essential item I carried. I sealed it in a plastic bag and carried it in my pack with my journal.

Whenever I hit a low, I pulled it out. It was like hearing their voices, reminding me why I started this journey in the first place.

March 14–15, 2012 – Wednesday & Thursday (Zero Days)

We rested for two days, letting our bodies begin to heal. Michael needed the time for his Achilles. I used the time to clean my gear, reevaluate my pack, and reconnect with my family. I caught up with both of my sons, Nathan and Jarrod, on the phone. This was the longest I had ever been away from them. Their voices anchored me.

We also revisited our trail plan. Now that we had a clearer sense of our pace, we adjusted our food drop locations. Pam's basement became trail HQ, with ziplock bags of oatmeal, pre-packed meals, and trail mix lined up in rows. Five days of food meant five breakfasts, five dinners, five baggies of lunch snacks... and hopefully, a food box waiting at the end. The logistics were overwhelming sometimes, but breaking the AT into small, manageable chunks made it feel doable.

We used that second day to prepare for the next stretch—more storms were in the forecast. I bought a better poncho, a drop cloth for my pack, and ruthlessly pared down my gear again. The flip-phone charger didn't make the cut. My old flip phone could hold a charge for days anyway, and every ounce mattered.

Pam made meatloaf that night. Real, home-cooked food—nothing dehydrated or eaten with a plastic spork. I savored every bite. But despite the comfort, I couldn't ignore the anxiety creeping in. Twice that night, I woke up with a racing heart. I was physically ready to return to the trail... but mentally? I wasn't so sure.

So, I called Stephanie.

She didn't tell me what to do. She never tried to fix it. She just listened—and then reminded me that I had everything I needed to keep going. She reminded me of who I was.

By the time I hung up, I was breathing easier. I finally slept.

Chapter 2

Finding a Stride

North Carolina / Tennessee

March 16, 2012 - Friday

We kicked off the day with an early hot breakfast, then all piled into Pam's SUV for the three-hour drive back to Hiawassee at Dick's Creek Gap. As soon as we got there, we hit the AT and knocked out nine miles to Bly Gap, just inside North Carolina, which was our second state! The AT runs through 14 states from start to finish, and it felt good to have our first one behind us.

The hike was more pleasant than the earlier stretches and still had plenty of ups and downs, but the slopes were more gradual this time. Michael stuck with me most of the way because he wanted to slow his pace and protect his healing ankle tendon. We reached Bly Gap around 4:00 p.m. after about five hours on the trail and set up camp. Other hikers trickled in around 5:00 p.m., and by 7:00 p.m. it had started raining and turned cold.

The rain kept us trapped in our tents with not much to do. I tried calling Stephanie, but there was no cell service. Dinner was ramen noodles and tuna, made a bit better thanks to the dehydrated veggies Pam had packed for us. With nothing else to do, we called it an early night and listened to the rain drum steadily on the tent.

March 17, 2012 - Saturday

 I woke up surprisingly well-rested after the rainy night, even with the hard ground under the tent. Those two rest days had done wonders for my mood and my body. I started the morning with my usual routine: a quick breakfast of packaged oatmeal and then packing up my gear.

The first part of the day's hike was mostly uphill and pretty rough, but we kept a good pace and made it to our planned stop at Standing Indian Shelter, by about 1:30 p.m.

We set up the tent and spent the afternoon just taking it easy. Michael found a Western novel in the shelter and got lost in that for a few hours. I was excited to finally have a cell signal and managed to reach Stephanie to give her an update on our progress, but the reception was terrible, and we got cut off. I couldn't get the signal back after that.

After I fixed dinner, more hikers started showing up. I met Hat, Medicine Man, Chad, Turtle, and a few others. A couple of them admitted they'd taken some side trails or shortcuts called "blue-blazing."

I've always been a purist about the AT. I wanted to hike every single, white-blazed mile without skipping a thing, but I kept that opinion to myself. Everyone's entitled to hike their own hike.

We built a campfire and sat around talking. Some of the guys were smoking, something I never got into. The conversation was good, but Turtle didn't really fit in. He was a little guy dressed all in green, looking just like a turtle with his pack on. He kept smoking weed and bragging about carrying a .45, saying he'd shoot any bear right between the eyes. I was pretty sure weapons were illegal in federal parklands, including the AT. Later, I heard a rumor that the authorities caught up with him and pulled him off the trail for having that gun.

March 18, 2012 - Sunday

Michael and I were up and out by 8:30 a.m., slipping easily into our usual morning routine of breakfast, then a quick pack up, and hit the trail. We were moving well, feeling rested and mostly healed up. The shelter had been at about 4,760 feet, but today we had to get over Standing Indian Mountain at 5,498 feet. It was a pretty steep 700-foot climb in just a mile and a half. I'd dreaded it, but the early climb turned out to be better than I'd feared, and we made it to Carter Gap Shelter by lunchtime. We stopped to eat there and saw August and three women we'd run into a few times before.

Most days, everybody hikes at their own pace, sometimes alone, sometimes spread out, but the shelters and campsites always seem to gather us back up. It's funny how you keep bumping into the same people. Someone might pass you one day, then drop off the trail to resupply or rest, and suddenly you're ahead again.

It happens over and over, even in a single day. Hikers passing each other, stopping, leapfrogging down the trail. We called it "yo-yoing."

After lunch, we headed on toward Betty Creek, planning to camp there, but it didn't feel like a good spot, so we decided to push on to Big Spring Shelter instead. That meant tackling Albert Mountain, which is infamous for its difficult 0.2-mile rock scramble, according to the Thru-hiker's Handbook.

The Center for Appalachian Trail Studies puts out the Handbook and other guides for hikers, and Stephanie had picked up an old copy to follow along while I was out here. She didn't realize the trail shifts a bit every year, so what she was reading wasn't exactly what I was hiking, but it helped her feel connected to me, especially when I went days without a signal. Sometimes when I did get through, the signal was so poor that I barely said more than where I was or what I needed for the next supply box.

That climb up Albert Mountain was nearly straight up. I was drenched in sweat, but when I reached the top, the view made every step worth it. We got to Big Spring Shelter around 4:15 p.m. after more than 14 miles for the day. We set up our sleeping bags and ate dinner. Chad and another hiker stayed at the shelter near us, but the rest of the group we'd been loosely hiking with camped farther up the trail, as there was not much flat ground for tents here.

We turned in after a short campfire, lights out by 8:30 p.m. Out here, they say 9:00 p.m. is "hiker midnight" because by then, everyone's zipped up in their bags and half asleep. Sleep didn't come easily for me again, though. Just as my body would finally stop, my mind would crank up. I managed to calm my thoughts a bit by pulling out the card my co-workers had given me before I left. I also thought about the emails people sent through the list Stephanie started, so she could keep everyone updated on my hike, and finally relaxed enough to sleep.

March 19, 2012 — Monday

We hit the trail around 8:30 a.m. The plan was to hike to Winding Stair Gap and meet Michael's brother, Andy, who was making the long drive from Knoxville to personally deliver our next food drop package.

It felt good to move. The morning air was crisp, the trail dry from the storm's passing, and our pace steady. We made it to Winding Stair Gap by 12:30 p.m., a full hour ahead of schedule.

I didn't know until then that De Soto may have passed through this very area, his expedition unknowingly tracing what would become our footpath centuries later.

Andy's route was detoured by construction and a traffic ticket, so he showed up a couple of hours late, but no one minded. It was good to see him, and we quickly swapped out our trash for resupply, reorganized our packs, and headed off for Siler Bald Shelter.

Even with the delay, we made it to the shelter by 5:30 p.m., another solid 14-mile day. For someone aiming to average 12 miles a day over six months, this was a promising sign. But the terrain at camp didn't do us any favors. The clearing was scenic but hardly level. We pitched the tent on the least-sloped spot we could find, cooked up some dinner, and I walked down to the creek to freshen up.

Keeping clean out here is optimistic at best. Soap fouls the drinking water, and bathing opportunities are few and far between. I half-joked that I have to keep hiking just to stay ahead of my own stink. Fortunately, everyone smells equally terrible out here, so no one notices.

That night, I talked with a couple of section hikers, T.J. and Brian. We swapped stories. They were good guys, friendly, curious. We talked gear, and Brian gave me the rundown on hammock tents, which sounded efficient but a bit drafty for my taste. There's something comforting about shelter walls, even thin nylon ones.

Sleep came early, as always, but not deeply. The ground sloped just enough to keep me aware of it all night.

March 20, 2012 — Tuesday

We broke camp earlier than usual. Michael took down the tent for a change, and I appreciated the switch. But a few miles in, I noticed I was missing my wallet.

Panic flared in my gut, but there wasn't much I could do. We had miles to cover, and turning back wasn't an option. I hiked on, distracted, worried about losing my ID and credit card, although I had some emergency cash stashed in my pack, so I'd be OK with money.

The climbs were relentless today, the kind that make you feel every ounce of your pack and every year of your age. We reached Cold Spring Shelter, one of the oldest on the AT, by a little after 3 p.m. The place was already full, so we found a patch of uneven ground nearby and pitched the tent again.

When we unrolled it, there was the wallet, tucked into the folds like a stowaway. Relief doesn't begin to cover it.

Later, I got a bit of cell service and called Larissa. She told me she was expecting another boy, my third grandson. My heart swelled, and then broke a little, too. I missed my family fiercely. I'd always been the one holding things together as the provider, protector, and the solid rock. Walking away from that, even temporarily, felt selfish. But I also knew my kids were grown now. They had their own paths to walk. I was proud of them.

My other daughter, Sarah, had moved into my house with my first grandson Cameron, while I was away. He needed more educational support, and the suburban school district near my place could offer that. Knowing they were safe and settled helped ease the guilt a little. Still, the ache lingered.

This trail was changing me, but part of that change, I realized, was learning how to let go.

March 21, 2012 — Wednesday

We were on the move by 8 a.m. The morning mist was so thick it felt like walking through clouds. I had hoped for some scenic ridge shots, but the fog had other plans.

By early afternoon, we reached the Nantahala Outdoor Center (NOC). Our next supply box had just arrived, thanks to Pam's perfect timing. We ordered greasy patty melts and onion rings—our stomachs rejoiced... and then revolted. After weeks of oatmeal and jerky, our systems weren't sure what to do with fried food.

Instead of staying at the hostel, we pushed on. In hindsight, that was a mistake. We hiked for a total of 14 miles and ended up camping alone near Grassy Gap. There were no other hikers around, probably because there wasn't a nearby water source. We had filled up at the NOC, but it still felt unsettling to be so isolated.

There was a massive rock formation near the site, craggy and hollow like something out of a fantasy novel. Michael had to inspect it before he could sleep. That night, for reasons I can't explain, I slept well.

March 22, 2012 — Thursday

We got moving by 7:50 a.m. Cheoah Bald and Swim Bald were no joke; those climbs burned. Up was tough on the lungs, down was murder on the knees. I'd hoped my body would adapt by now, but the daily pain reminded me otherwise. Still, we kept walking.

At Stecoah Gap, we experienced our first real "trail magic". A man was handing out fruit and drinks to any passing hiker. No strings. Just kindness. After he left, a woman and her family offered us sandwiches. Simple food had never tasted so good.

The Trail has a way of humbling you and then lifting you up just when you think you can't go on.

That night, we stayed at Brown Fork Gap Shelter. There was a good crowd, and the conversation flowed easily. Some were heading to Fontana Dam shelter next, like us. It felt good to be among people again.

And, believe it or not, they had the nicest privy I'd seen on the trail. You learn to appreciate strange things out here.

March 23, 2012 — Friday

Rain overnight, again. We were lucky to be in the shelter. Everything stayed dry.

The hike was typical ups, downs, and everything in between. Michael, ever the faster hiker, made it to Fontana Dam ahead of me and caught a shuttle into the village to grab our supply box. I rolled in by 1:30 p.m. and we divvied up the goods before heading to the shelter.

The Fontana Dam Shelter, nicknamed the "Fontana Hilton" by appreciative hikers, was luxurious by trail standards. It had a shower! I actually scrubbed myself and washed one outfit. It didn't erase the funk entirely, but it helped.

There were 24 bunks and a fireplace. We sat around it, swapping stories until the embers dimmed. I got a call through to Stephanie that evening. Just hearing her voice helped reset something in me. This trail is hard, but I could feel my body growing stronger. Slowly.

A thunderstorm rolled in around 1 a.m., but I was dry, warm, and grateful.

March 24, 2012 — Saturday – (Zero Day)

I was up early, savoring the view of Lake Fontana while Michael slept in. We'd planned a Zero day, and the "Fontana Hilton" had set the tone for comfort. Once Michael emerged, we caught a ride into Fontana Village and waited for our motel room to be ready.

We passed the time doing laundry with a couple of hikers we'd met earlier. There's something oddly satisfying about clean socks. Afterward, we organized food from our supply box and caught a hot meal at the diner. I even stayed up to watch some March Madness and cheer on Syracuse. They won, and I went to bed at the scandalously late hour of 10:30 p.m. The motel bed was flat—and I mean *really* flat. I hadn't realized how much I missed level sleeping until then.

March 25, 2012 — Sunday

Despite the "late" night, we were up early and caught a shuttle back to the trail. Our driver was an older gentleman with a Southern drawl so thick even Michael couldn't make sense of it. But he was kind and cheap at just $2, and we were grateful for the ride.

By 9 a.m., we were back on the AT, climbing into the Great Smoky Mountains. Permits were required, so we filled out the forms at a quiet kiosk and pinned half to our packs.

Ridge-running through the Smokies was stunning. One side of the trail showed endless forest, the other gave glimpses of roads and towns, civilization always close, but never quite within reach.

We made it to Russell Field Shelter, 13.8 miles in. We felt strong enough to have gone farther, but Smokies rules meant you had to stay in designated shelters, and we wouldn't have made it to the next one. Dinner was a disaster. Red beans and rice with meat that had gone bad. I ate it anyway. Hunger wins.

That night, I curled up under a skylight with a cheap paperback I'd grabbed at the laundromat. Around me were older hikers, like me. We shared stories of families, of past hikes, of reasons for being here. For a while, the ache of missing home faded, replaced by this odd little brotherhood built on aching knees and trust.

Even with the wind howling, I slept well.

March 26, 2012 – Monday

Michael surprised me by joining me for breakfast. Usually, he wasn't much for eating first thing. A granola bar or two if anything, but something was shifting.

He was getting the hiker's appetite that I seemed to have had all along.

We hit the trail by 8 a.m., winding our way through the Smokies. It was all ups and downs now, and my arthritic knees were starting to feel it. I gave in and took some ibuprofen, or "Vitamin I" as hikers jokingly call it. I used to pride myself on not taking anything. Back in my school days, I was an athlete and kept a strict line when it came to drugs of any kind. Even aspirin was rare for me. But the Appalachian Trail was humbling. I found myself reaching for that little white pill bottle more and more often as the days wore on.

Still, despite the pain, I was in good enough shape by now to start truly appreciating the trail around me. The Smokies were stunning with the moody skies, mist hanging in the valleys, and not a road or power line in sight. We were walking along high ridges with sweeping views in every direction, completely removed from civilization. That sense of isolation was oddly comforting.

We passed a couple of shelters throughout the day and finally settled at Silers Bald Shelter after a solid 14.7 miles. This shelter felt downright luxurious! It had two levels, a skylight, a fireplace, and a tarp covering the front to block the wind. Compared to the usual open-faced, three-wall shelters, this was the Ritz.

There were about 20 people already there. Most were respectful, but a couple of weekenders had brought a tablet and were watching movies, loudly. I was quietly fuming. To me, the wilderness is sacred. Watching movies in a shelter in the middle of a national park felt like an affront. That same guy ended up snoring like a freight train all night, but thankfully, I had my trusty earplugs. Dinner was a pouch of chicken and rice, and despite the distractions, I got some sleep. Rain tapped on the tarp as I drifted off. I was grateful to be under a roof.

The next day was **Tuesday, March 27**. We were about three weeks into our trek.

We were on the trail by 8 a.m. again, climbing through rock-strewn paths and into a different world with shorter trees, moss-covered boulders, and thinner air. By 11:15 a.m., we reached Clingmans Dome, the highest point on the entire Appalachian Trail at 6,643 feet.

It was a big moment.

As we approached the top, I was hit with a strange mix of emotions. There was a road up there, and a parking lot full of tourists in flip-flops, snapping photos, smelling like soap and dryer sheets. We must've looked like wild men, all sweaty, dirty, and worn thin from the climb. But we had *earned* that view.

The 360-degree vista from the observation tower was unforgettable. Blue ridges rolled out in every direction, layered in that mysterious haze that gives the Smokies their name. It was surreal, almost dreamlike.

This wasn't my first time here. Years ago, I'd come with my whole family on a trip to visit my sister Pam. All four kids had still lived at home, and we'd driven through the Smokies, parked at Clingmans Dome, and clambered up to the tower, just like the tourists we saw today. I remember seeing real thru-hikers back then, heavy packs and sun-worn faces. I'd stared at them with a sort of reverence, secretly wishing I could do what they were doing. But I had a family, a job, and responsibilities. The idea of leaving it all behind for months felt impossible.

And yet, here I was. At age 60. Standing where I once stood as a tourist, but now as a hiker—*a thru-hiker*. Even if my journey ended here, I had done something I never thought I could. I had already realized a lifelong dream.

After soaking in the moment, we made it a light day and only hiked another 4 miles to Mount Collins Shelter. We needed the rest. The shelter was packed, so some hikers tented nearby. I tried and failed to get a text out to Stephanie, as there was no signal at that elevation. I chatted for a bit with a father from Minnesota and his two sons, who were out for a five-day hike. It reminded me of my own family and how much I missed them.

That night was cold, probably 20 degrees cooler than the valleys below, and the zipper on my sleeping bag broke, letting in the chill. I didn't sleep much. There was always *something* getting in the way of a good night's sleep.

March 28, 2012 – Wednesday

We awoke and started hiking again around 8 a.m., as had become our routine. The morning was peaceful with a downhill walk through the pine forest to Newfound Gap. Tennessee! Our third state. The gap had a parking area, a privy, and thankfully, no movie-watching weekenders.

After a big climb out of the gap, the trail mellowed out with undulating ridge walks. But even those ridges could be intimidating. At 5,000 feet, the path narrowed and the drop-offs were steep. Wind picked up, fog swirled in and out. At times, the mist would spill over the trail like a waterfall made of clouds.

I was alone for a good stretch. Michael, always faster, had gone on ahead. As the trail dipped into a foggy tunnel beneath the trees, it felt like stepping into a cave or a fantasy world. I thought of *The Lord of the Rings*, of Mordor. Dark. Misty. Ancient.

I felt small.

The Smokies are vast. Far bigger than I had imagined, and I was just a speck walking through them. Every direction held hidden valleys, unseen trails. The enormity of it all left me awestruck. It was one of the most memorable days I would spend on the trail, a day photographs could never capture.

We reached Peck Shelter by 3:30 p.m. and were alone there for a little while. Later, other hikers arrived, including a red-haired woman named Glide. Something about her reminded me of my daughter Sarah. I missed my kids. I missed Stephanie. I was living my dream, yes, but that dream had a cost. I had never been away from home this long without family. Michael was a familiar face, but I felt responsible for him. He didn't need a father figure out here, just a hiking partner.

That night it rained again. The shelter filled with the steady patter on the roof. As I drifted off, warm in my broken sleeping bag, I felt the tug of home and the pull of the trail; they were two loves, impossible to hold at once.

March 29, 2012 – Thursday

The day began draped in a heavy gray fog. We set off, as usual, around 8 a.m., our boots muffled on the pine needle trail. There's a kind of hush in a pine forest that's hard to describe—soft, insulated, and peaceful. I always felt a sense of calm in the pines.

The scenery may have been less dramatic than the ridgelines and mountain vistas, but the silence felt like a balm.

That morning's hike took us over two mountains and along more fog-drenched ridges where the mist rolled like waterfalls off either side. At one point, I saw two deer drinking from a stream just off the trail. It's rare to see wildlife up close with all the clatter of boots and trekking poles, but the soft ground hushed our approach. For a moment, it felt like the forest had let us in on a secret.

After nearly 13 miles, we reached Cosby Knob Shelter just as the fog gave way to sunlight. It felt like a warm welcome. The shelter was full again—no surprise—but it was comfortable, and the quiet of the pine woods lingered in my bones. That night, I finally slept deeply. The kind of sleep that feels like being cradled by the trail itself.

March 30, 2012 – Friday

This was our last day in the Smokies. We left a bit after 8 a.m., climbing Mount Canmerer first thing. I always tried to plan our stops so the next morning's hike would begin with a climb. I was stronger with rested legs and fewer aches. Better to tackle a mountain early than drag up one at day's end.

As we descended toward Davenport Gap, spring greeted us like an old friend. The cold forests gave way to bright green undergrowth and blooming wildflowers. A yellow-petaled plant with big leaves carpeted the forest floor. It felt like we were walking into a new season, both in the world and in ourselves.

Crossing the Pigeon River and I-40 marked the official end of the Smokies. It felt like a milestone. We stopped to resupply at the quirky Standing Bear Hostel, which was about as rustic and bare-bones as a hostel could get. The food options were limited, but we stocked up on what we could. On the way out, Michael spotted a rattlesnake curled just off the trail—the first I'd ever seen. Beautiful. Menacing. A reminder that we were still guests out here.

Then the skies opened. Rain turned to downpour as we climbed Snowbird Mountain, one of the balds with no tree cover—4,263 feet up and completely exposed. That's when the thunder started. I won't lie, it scared me. Michael ran ahead, disappearing into the storm. I didn't run. I just kept walking, slow and steady, half-thinking, *Well, if a lightning bolt wants me, I won't outrun it anyway.*

We hiked over 17 miles that day, our longest day yet. Soaked to the bone, we reached Groundhog Creek Shelter in the dark, squeezing into the lean-to with 14 other wet, miserable hikers—far more than it was built for. The rain let up just long enough for us to pitch our tent and eat something warm. No fire. No dry wood. We were cold and shivering. I wore my parka inside my sleeping bag, my usual pillow now my only warmth.

But I had a cell signal.

I called Stephanie. And just hearing her voice cut through the cold. It had been a long, silent week. She and Pam had been anxious. Michael had texted home earlier, so they knew we were alive, but I could tell she'd been waiting to *hear* from me. I started to tell her about the last few days, but got cut off when my uncharged flip phone finally died. I borrowed Michael's phone to call back.

We talked logistics, like how far we'd come: 244.7 miles in 23 days. Just over 10 miles per day, but we needed to average 12 if we wanted to finish the trail in one season. I hoped the pace would pick up now that the big mountains were behind us. We were almost out of our pre-packed food drops, but luckily, an Easter break was coming soon. Stephanie would fly back to Tennessee, and Pam would pick us up for the weekend. A brief return to family, food, and dry clothes.

Stephanie said I sounded upbeat. I was wet, tired, and cold, but yes, I was still filled with purpose. After the call, I climbed into the tent and wrapped myself in as tightly as I could with the broken zipper on my sleeping bag. The rain returned, tapping out its rhythm through the night.

March 31, 2012 – Saturday

After that freezing, damp night, I didn't get moving until after 9 a.m. Michael was still curled in his sleeping bag, so I headed out alone. It was a short day by choice—just 8.2 miles—but it was enough. There were lots of climbs, still blanketed in fog, and the trail tested us even on the shorter days.

Rain threatened all day, but to our amazement, it held off.

Midday, I found myself hiking across Max Patch. It's a grassy bald, with a panoramic view that stretches for miles in every direction. Michael caught up with me there. He slowed his pace and walked beside me for a while—a small gesture, but one that meant a lot.

We don't always say it out loud, but we were learning how to be trail companions, not just relatives.

When we reached Roaring Fork Shelter, we hung our soaked gear in the sun. The tent. Our clothes. Everything had that sour, wet hiker smell, but we were just glad to be drying out. The afternoon became a rare chance to rest and let our bodies repair.

That's when Video Joe arrived. A balding, talkative middle-aged guy with a camera and a mission: to document thru-hikers and assign trail names. Some hikers pick their own names, but often, the trail gives it to you. Joe asked what ours were. Michael didn't have one, and neither did I.

When I told him I was a birdwatcher and had always wanted to see an owl but had only heard them, never seen one, his eyes lit up.

"Hoot," he said. "That's your name."

And just like that, it felt right. "Hoot." A little silly, a little wise, maybe even a little unseen, like the owls I'd been chasing. It fit. I tried it on and decided to keep it.

Joe offered Michael a name, too, something about being a young rookie, but Michael declined. He'd stay "Michael," at least for now.

That night, Michael picked a campsite farther from the shelter. I stayed close, chatting with other hikers for a while before settling in. In the tent, we both dozed off early. Michael's sleeping bag kept sliding on the slight slope and bumping into me during the night, but I didn't mind much. It was one of those nights where discomfort just fades into the rhythm of trail life.

And now, I was Hoot. Still Greg, of course, but something new had taken root in me.

By **April 1st,** we had been on the Appalachian Trail long enough to create a rhythm. Every day was a simple routine of hiking, eating, resting, and moving again. It had all begun to feel normal, even soothing. Michael and I were still hiking separately most days, carving out space to process the miles in our own way.

That Sunday, I walked alone for nearly fifteen miles through pine forests, breathing in their resinous scent. I spotted a four-foot rat snake sunning itself on the trail—it didn't startle me. I was getting used to these encounters. The trail teaches you quickly what's worth fearing and what's just part of the wild.

I arrived early at the Deer Park Mountain Shelter, just before the wind shifted and the storm rolled in. The timing felt like grace.

Michael arrived later, carrying less enthusiasm than usual. He confessed, again, how hard the food situation was for him. He was losing more weight than he could afford. I began to worry—not just about his body, but his heart. Just like I missed my family, he seemed homesick, too. The trail was stripping us both down, and what was underneath was beginning to show.

The next morning, **April 2nd,** we walked the easy three miles into Hot Springs, North Carolina. It felt surreal to be in a real town again. We checked into a little place called Springbrook Cottages—clean, warm, and ours for a day. The Smoky Mountain Diner served up a hearty late lunch that was both cheap and good.

We showered, did laundry, and bought fresh supplies. We watched the NCAA championship in our room. Luckily, there were cell phone chargers left there by other hikers that fit my flip phone, so I was able to contact people once more. I called Stephanie and then Larissa to update them on my progress, and to ask for any emails to be sent by Easter so I could read them when I reached Pam's for our upcoming break. The town of Hot Springs caters to hikers, so we felt welcome and comfortable.

I talked to Stephanie on the phone. Her voice steadied me. She told me she was proud. I needed to hear it. I knew I was losing weight, but I was gaining strength in a way I hadn't felt in years. The idea of completing the whole trail in one season started to feel not just possible—but likely.

The next day, **April 3rd,** we set out from Allen Gap and climbed back into the hills. That day, something changed. I knew I could do this. At a gravel road crossing, we found a small house with a sign: "Thru-Hikers Welcome." Inside, a former hiker named Hercules and his wife Fal offered us a wonderful meal starting with a waffle, then stew, and finished with apple cobbler and ice cream. They'd walked this path before, and now they were giving back.

There were religious books and pamphlets available, and I picked up a paperback. I had not attended church since the hike began, because a priest had reassured me that church-going was not required on pilgrimages or travel like this. I felt that I was walking daily in "God's Cathedral" as I hiked the woods and mountains.

However, I looked forward to a spiritual evening read, and indeed enjoyed the book, although it came from a different branch of

Christianity than my Roman Catholic upbringing. Their kindness overwhelmed me. We left with full bellies and lighter spirits.

Later that afternoon, we crossed just shy of 20 miles in the rain. The shelter was full, so we pitched our tent in the drizzle, shivering into our sleeping bags. But I didn't mind. There was warmth in knowing we were earning our way, one mile at a time.

Wednesday, April 4th followed a similar pattern, and on **April 5th**, we hit a particularly rough patch with a series of climbs and a long descent into Sam's Gap. My knees screamed on the downhills, but I pushed through. At the bottom, a man waved us over and handed us hot hash browns, scrambled eggs, and orange wedges. Trail magic, again. It's the kind of generosity that humbles you. I realized that survival on the trail wasn't always about pushing hard. Sometimes it was about receiving what was offered.

That night, we camped at Low Gap. Two Barred owls circled above our tent, calling out into the night. My first owl sighting! "Who cooks for you?" they asked in their wild, echoing voices. It felt like a sign. I had taken the trail name "Hoot," and in that moment, I felt I had finally earned the name.

The next day, **Friday, April 6th**, we pushed on through dense fog over Big Bald and Little Bald. Visibility was so bad we had to concentrate hard on looking for the white blazes that mark the AT. My boots were caked in mud, and I slipped more than once. But at Spivey Gap, right on schedule, Pam and Les pulled up in their car. They drove us back to their home in Knoxville. I climbed up the stairs from the garage, dropped my pack, turned, and there she was—Stephanie.

I can't describe what it meant to see her. Her arms wrapped around me, and I felt I was home. I was also proud. I had survived. I had made it through the first month and over 300 miles, and I still had more to give. I was down 18 pounds, but I'd never felt stronger. My heart was steady. My legs were sturdy. I was no longer just walking the trail—I was part of it.

The next morning, **April 7th**, Stephanie and I sat at the breakfast table, laughing. She took me to a nearby outfitter and bought me a new sleeping bag—one rated for colder nights, and with a strong zipper. As we walked through the aisles, she asked me something that stayed with me. "Are you just trying to survive out there … or are you paying attention?"

It was a good question. On the trail, it's easy to put your head down and just push through the pain, the hunger, the loneliness. But survival isn't only about enduring. It's about noticing. The owls. The pine needles. The faces of strangers who feed you. The voice on the phone that reminds you why you started.

I made a promise to myself that day. I would keep walking. But I would also look up. I would pay attention. I would remember that the trail gives as much as it takes—if you let it.

April 8, 2012 – Easter Sunday (Zero)

I slept in until almost 8:00 a.m. that morning, unheard of for me on the trail. By that hour, I'd normally have already eaten, packed up, and been miles into the day's hike. But this was Easter, and I was with family.

Pam, as always, made a wonderful breakfast. We all sat together, talking and laughing around the table. It was comforting, but there was a tug inside me. I had never missed Easter service before. Not once. The absence of church that morning weighed heavily on my heart.

Stephanie helped type up my handwritten journal so far, just in case it got lost—and emailed a copy to herself for safekeeping. That simple act meant a lot to me. My journal was more than just notes; it was my record, my companion, a chronicle of something that had come to feel larger than myself.

Later, I took a nap, then called my son Jarrod. We caught up, and I got to speak with his wife, Colleen and her mom, Phyllis, too. Phyllis had been following my hike from afar—reading the updates Stephanie sent out. I still couldn't quite wrap my head around the fact that people cared about my journey. Every time someone said they were rooting for me, it humbled me. I felt guilty, sometimes—like this hike was selfish, indulgent, unproductive. But the messages Stephanie had collected and read to me that day … they broke something open in me. I wept.

Notes from family, friends, old coworkers—even strangers—touched something deep. They believed in me, and maybe, I thought, it was time I did too.

I also called my youngest daughter, Sarah. We talked for a while, and I got to hear my grandson Cameron's voice, my first grandchild. After Peggy died, it was Cameron who kept me going. He gave me something to wake up for in those early days of grief. Sarah told me the house was fine, the neighborhood too.

She assured me everything was taken care of, that I didn't need to worry. But of course, I did. I missed them terribly. I missed all of them.

We were a close family. Holidays like Easter were always spent together. It physically hurt to be away from them now.

Pam didn't let the holiday pass without celebration, though. She made a full Easter dinner: ham, potatoes, asparagus, corn muffins, and cheesecake. I wrote every bite down in my journal. I'd always loved food, but after burning thousands of calories on the trail each day, food had become something almost sacred. That day, we also assembled trail food packages to send ahead to future resupply points. The hike would resume the next morning.

That evening, I trimmed my beard, leaving most of it to keep warm in the higher elevations. Michael shaved his off completely—he would be the Best Man in a wedding coming up and didn't want to look too rough in the pictures. Stephanie and I sat with Pam and Les, watching TV, but our eyes kept drifting to each other. We both knew what was coming: another long stretch apart.

April 9, 2012 – Monday

That morning, we loaded up our gear and prepped to head back to the trail. I could feel myself shifting into my hiker mode. Greg was gently retreating as "Hoot" came forward. Hoot needed to be focused. Efficient. Ready. Greg loved Stephanie and wanted to linger, but Hoot had miles to cover.

Pam's SUV refused to start, and Les had already left for work, so Stephanie's rental car saved the day. Somehow, we squeezed four adults and two fully loaded packs into it. Two hours later, we were back at Spivey Gap. I kissed Stephanie, hugged Pam, and then we were gone again—back into the bare, leafless forest that had become our new home.

It was a good day for hiking, crisp but dry. We reached Erwin, Tennessee, where the Appalachian Trail skirts the Nolichucky River. It was tempting to stop in town, but we felt strong from the break and kept pushing. Fifteen miles later, we arrived at Curly Maple Gap Shelter and ate sandwiches we'd packed from Pam's. Fresh food—what a luxury.

That night, we met August again, the strong, chatty, ex-Army guy we'd first seen near Springer Mountain. The trail was his community, and he was one of the few Black hikers we encountered. His campfire and storytelling became a kind of tradition at shelters.

We also met Magpie and Kitty. Magpie was slower, but steady, something I respected. I'd later learn she had health issues, but her determination was unwavering. Kitty was quick, sharp, and made a strong impression. Serious hikers, both of them.

April 10, 2012 – Tuesday

Back to the grind. Up early, oatmeal and tea for me, dried bars for Michael. We were hiking by 8 a.m.

It was a rough day; over 12 miles of roots, rocks, and relentless climbs. My knees hated me for it. By the time we reached Cherry Gap Shelter, I was exhausted. Michael preferred the privacy of the tent, so we pitched it instead of sleeping in the rodent-friendly shelter.

We ran into a familiar face, Atlas, now going by Full Service. Trail names evolved, much like the hikers who carried them.

Still no cell signal. I missed the connection with my family, and to Stephanie. The cold set in again. The wind howled through the forest like a freight train. It always seemed to wait for us.

April 11, 2012 – Wednesday

I was up and out by 8 a.m. Michael and I hiked separately most of the time now, only really sharing a tent and stove at night. The solitude suited me, though. It gave me space to think.

We pushed to Roan High Knob Shelter after learning that Ash Gap had no reliable water. That climb—6,285 feet—was a killer, especially at the end of the day. The pine forest at the summit looked like something out of a fairy tale. Beautiful, haunting … and cold.

The shelter was more like a cabin, which was a blessing, but it didn't stop my water bottles from freezing. I spent the night shivering in every layer I had, barely sleeping. My nose kept freezing when I poked it out for air. Worst night on the trail yet.

April 12, 2012 – Thursday

I couldn't wait for sunrise. I was dressed, packed, and on the move by 7:00 a.m., desperate to get warm. No breakfast—my water was still frozen. The trail downhill was wide, almost like a real path, and I relished the simplicity of it.

Michael caught up later, and we hiked the Balds together. Finally, we stopped at Stan Murray Shelter and made a proper breakfast. No privy, though—just the woods.

We had planned to finish the section tomorrow, but realized we could reach Route 19E by evening. Pam agreed to meet us, despite the three-hour drive. My sister was a saint.

Near the trailhead, a kind man had set up trail magic: chili, fruit, cupcakes, soda. We feasted and waited for Pam. On the ride back, Michael told me he wanted to hike solo from now on. I cycled through disappointment, anger, and then acceptance. Everyone hikes their own hike. I would not let this deter me; after all, we had pretty much been hiking apart. In a way, this would give me the freedom I didn't realize I wanted.

That night, I collapsed into the warmth of Pam's guest bed, clean and fed, grateful and unsure about the road ahead.

Interlude – April 13, 14 – Zero Days

Chapter 3

The Hiker Routine

Tennessee / Virginia / West Virginia

April 15, 2012 – Sunday

After Les made breakfast, we had the car packed by 8:45 a.m. and were on our way back to Route 19E. It was late morning, about 11:15 a.m., when we arrived at the trailhead. We said our goodbyes, and I tried not to linger. The longer I stood there, the harder it would be to go. After one last hug, I turned and started down the Appalachian Trail again.

The walk to Mountaineer Shelter was just under nine miles. I got there around 3 p.m., still carrying some of the warmth from the morning with me.

For dinner, I tried one of the more expensive trail meals Pam had bought at the outfitter where I purchased my tent. It was better than I expected, comfort in a pouch.

That evening, I pulled out the small religious book I'd picked up a couple of weeks ago at the log cabin where Hercules and Fal had offered trail magic. I read a few pages, letting the quiet of the shelter settle over me, and planned out the next day's miles.

Now that I was hiking alone, I decided to sleep in the shelter. It felt strange at first, but good to be among other hikers again. Dame Quixote, a female hiker, was easy to talk to. Rhino, short for Reinhold, was a tall, athletic-looking German and John, another hiker, rounded out the evening's company.

We traded trail stories until it was time to sleep.

That night, bundled in my sleeping bag inside the shelter, I finally slept deeply.

April 16, 2012 - Monday

Without a tent to pack, I was up and moving by 7:35 a.m., earlier than usual.

My goal for the day was ambitious: 17.5 miles to Laurel Fork Shelter. On the map, it looked manageable. Aside from the climb over White Rocks Mountain, it seemed mostly flat. But the trail had other ideas.

The day turned into a rollercoaster of ups and downs, and the heat hit me hard at lower elevations. Just a few days ago, I'd been freezing on Roan Mountain, now I was sweating under the sun at 2,000 feet. The stretch near Laurel Fork Falls was beautiful. I stopped to take pictures of the falls, lingering on one view that I later framed and hung at home.

The approach trail to the shelter was terrible, with a lot of rocks, although it was well marked.

Shelters were often off the main trail and reached by a side trail. This added miles to the hike that didn't "count" as AT mileage.

Whenever I could, I picked spots close to the main trail to save wear and tear on my feet and legs!

Exhausted, I set up my new single-person tent, made dinner, and sent a few quick texts to Stephanie and Jarrod. Then I went to the top of a nearby waterfall to fetch water. That's when the unexpected happened: I stepped onto a wet, mossy rock and slipped. In an instant, I was in the rushing water, headed toward a hundred-foot drop. Pure instinct made me grab an exposed tree root, and I clung to it with everything I had. My heart pounded as I hauled myself out, shaking.

If I'd been wearing my pack, I doubt I would've made it. Standing there dripping, I swore to myself I'd never walk on wet rocks again.

Mike showed up at the same campsite, having kept the same pace, and we each pitched our separate tents. I found I enjoyed my new privacy and the fact that I could get up without disturbing anyone else. It was slightly humorous that we still kept the same total mileage even after hiking solo.

April 17, 2012 – Tuesday

I was on the trail by 7:40 a.m. The sun rose earlier each day, and so did I. The morning began with a steep climb up to Pond Flats.

From there, the trail dropped down to Watauga Lake. I stopped at a quiet little beach, took off my shoes, and soaked my feet in the cool water while eating lunch, then continued around the lake toward Watauga Lake.

The dam itself was massive, one of the tallest earth-filled hydroelectric dams when it was built in the 1940s.

This part of the trail was fairly easy, with pleasant scenery, making it a lot of fun. After passing the dam, the AT rose uphill toward Iron Mountain. It wasn't a difficult climb, but I was tired from the earlier climb, and it was a long day of over 15 miles. I was happy to reach Vandeventer Shelter just in time to beat the rain and decided to stay there for the night.

It was an old shelter, and I hoped there weren't too many critters around. Out back there was an overlook where I could see Watauga Valley and the town of Butler, TN, near the lake. I took a picture when the rain cleared a bit, and a rainbow shone in the distance. At night, the lights of the town below eerily sparkled through the misty rain like a constellation on the ground.

Several older guys in their 50s stopped at the shelter. There were jokes written on the walls of the old shelter, and one of the hikers started a hilarious series of ridiculous jokes to keep everyone laughing. The air cooled considerably with the rain, which continued all night. Again, I found myself sleeping well, quite a change from before.

April 18, 2012 – Wednesday

The morning broke gray, heavy with rain. I sat in my sleeping bag, the patter on the shelter roof a steady drumbeat daring me to stay put. I gave it an hour, while I ate breakfast, hoping for a break in the weather. None came.

So, I did what you have to do out there sometimes; I put my head down and walked.

When it rained, I moved fast. That morning, I covered seven miles in three hours without even realizing it. I didn't see much of the scenery, just a blur of dripping leaves and slick rocks, but I broke my personal record that day: 22.7 miles.

A hiker named Houdini caught up with me for the last stretch, and his steady encouragement pushed me through the fatigue.

At Abingdon Shelter, I saw Tarzan, again. I was honored when Tarzan complimented me on my pace, telling me "It was hard for me today and I'm a marathon runner." The encouragement of Houdini and Tarzan gave me a huge boost. That night, I fell asleep smiling despite the miserable, wet weather.

April 19, 2012 – Thursday

The next day brought me to Virginia, the fourth state of my hike. Mile marker 296.7. Because of the hefty hike the previous day, I had an easy 10.2-mile hike to Damascus, making excellent time by covering the distance in only 3.5 hours.

I found Damascus to be a nice little town that catered to hikers and cyclists. The AT continued right up Main Street (Route 58) in town, so it was easy for me to stop at the Post Office on the way. I picked up the Virginia maps and food supplies that Stephanie had sent me there, and mailed back to her the maps of Tennessee and North Carolina I no longer needed.

Back out on Main Street, I noticed that the trail was demarcated with bricks. A story was that these could be "purchased" as a fundraiser for the AT. Damascus also calls itself "Trail Town USA" and is the site of an annual hiker celebration called Trail Days. Unfortunately, I was too early in the year for that June festival, but I enjoyed hiking through the pretty town.

I got a room at a hostel called Dave's Place, did laundry, took a shower — dingy and small shower stall, but heavenly to be clean — and shopped for some fresh food to supplement the ziplock bags of dried fare. At the laundry, I met Houdini again, and we ended up sharing the room to split the cost. My hiker's appetite couldn't resist an all-you-can-eat pizza buffet nearby, and while I was there, Mike came in as well. He ate too much, too fast, with ill effects. I had no such problem, but I felt that Virginia pizza compared poorly with my beloved city of Buffalo's many pizza eateries.

Despite Damascus being fairly small, I had heard there was a lot to do, but I was just too tired to take advantage of it. Another hostel in town was supposed to be a party hub, and Michael was staying there, but I preferred the quiet of Dave's Place.

Returning after dinner, I ran into a few more hikers I recognized, including Gunrunner and the young woman named Blue, for the blue shorts she wore, and we all chatted for a while. I had met Blue at Springer Mountain, and off and on throughout the hike, but I had never seen her with her hair down. Seeing her flowing golden hair now reminded me of my first wife, Peggy, at that same age.

I finished my evening by calling Stephanie, letting her know how pleased I was that my knees weren't hurting as much and that I was traveling much faster and farther. The uphill climbs were still difficult, especially when carrying several days of food, but I noticed that I was starting earlier in the day and finishing later without ill effects. I stayed up until almost 10 p.m., then crawled into my sleeping bag on the hard pallet. This was the first hostel I had stayed in during the hike, as any Zero days before I had spent taking a break at Pam's. The bed was uncomfortable, but I was able to sleep fairly well.

April 20, 2012 – Friday

Habit woke me early, but instead of cooking another packet of oatmeal on my little stove, I walked to the nearby Cowboy Exxon for their blueberry pancakes. They didn't live up to the hype, but the calories were enough to heave on my pack, say goodbye to Houdini, and hit the road back to the trail by 7:30 a.m.

The walk was OK, no rain, a well-marked trail, and climbs that weren't too steep. I was carrying six days of food, about 50 pounds, to get through a mountainous stretch before cold weather hit. The AT paralleled the Virginia Creeper bike trail, an easy rails-to-trails path that tempted some to skip the harder, white-blazed miles. For me, missing even an inch of the AT felt like cheating, though I couldn't help imagining how nice that easier path might be.

April 21, 2012 – Saturday

I reached Lost Mountain Shelter in seven hours and stopped, preferring to set up before dark. Blue was there with Maine-iac, Phoenix, and Indiana—young, energetic hikers drawing an AT-themed Monopoly board on the shelter floor. Mike showed up and stayed too. The laughter and chatter made me wish I could borrow some of their energy. I ate and turned in by 8:15 p.m., though the game went on until hiker midnight at 9 p.m.

In the morning, I was on the trail before most, walking through budding rhododendrons, my "rhododendron forest."

Blue flew past me before the climbs began: Whitetop Mountain at over 5,000 feet, then Mt. Rogers, Virginia's highest at 5,728 feet, though the AT skirted the summit. Past the treeless meadows of Grayson Highlands, I reached Wise Shelter after 17.3 cold, rainy miles.

Inside were Plus-Two, Rainbow, Unbreakable, and No Trace—friendly hikers I'd cross paths with again. I climbed a huge rock to call Stephanie, but lost the signal mid-sentence and couldn't get it back, leaving her with a cliffhanger for days.

That night, just as we settled in, wild ponies wandered up. Small, soft-coated, with long, thick manes, they nosed around for handouts. One tried to grab a water bottle. This was the last part of the park to see them, and we were thrilled. They came back in the middle of the night and again at sunrise, as if to say goodbye.

April 22, 2012 – Sunday

The ponies were still lingering in my mind when I woke, their soft noses and gentle curiosity a stark contrast to the morning that greeted me: cold, foggy, and wet. I ate quickly, packed up, and started down the trail before my body could protest. Just past the shelter, the Grayson Highlands ended at a fence built to keep the ponies in. There was no gate, only wooden steps to climb over, and then it was just me, the rain, and the rocks.

It was the kind of rain that seeps into you; quiet, persistent. I lowered my head and walked hard, letting my body fall into a rhythm. Nine hours later, I stumbled into Trimpi Shelter after 20 miles, my legs humming from the effort.

Four of my new trail friends were already there. Trimpi had a fireplace, a rare luxury, and soon the scent of smoke filled the room as we dried our gear. That night I claimed a spot near the fire and, as usual, woke often. Each time, I added a stick or two to keep the flames alive for all of us. The shelter was different from the usual three-sided lean-to; four full walls, a door-sized opening in the fourth side, and bunks stacked two high for sixteen hikers. Between the fire's warmth and the quiet breathing of friends, the cold couldn't touch me.

April 23, 2012 – Monday

I awoke at 6:15 a.m., later than usual, and for once I wasn't the first one on the trail. Outside, the picnic table glistened under a thin sheet of ice. I caught up to the others quickly, but the weather had other plans.

By mid-morning, snowflakes drifted down, turning the air sharp and the trail slick. Thankfully, all my clothes had dried overnight. That relief didn't last long.

Plus-Two and I outpaced Rainbow, No Trace, and Unbreakable, making it to Partnership Shelter by 11 a.m. The Mt. Rogers Visitor Center was nearby, and I ducked in to buy gloves. The only pair they had was a stretchy women's size, but they fit, and that was all that mattered. I'd sent my winter gloves back to Stephanie with a load of used maps just a week ago, thinking winter was behind me.

We pressed on, climbing Glade Mountain. That's when the snow turned mean, the wind roaring across the ridge. My poncho ballooned into a sail, tugging me sideways, threatening to toss me off balance. It stopped being about hiking and became survival. When we reached the road to Atkins, VA, we didn't hesitate; we headed for town.

From the ridge, the valley below had looked snow-free, and sure enough, as we dropped in elevation, the storm vanished. Behind us, the mountains were still streaked white. After 22 miles, the Relax Inn felt like an oasis, even if the door barely closed and the shower leaked.

Dinner was at The Barn, a restaurant that was literally a barn. I called Stephanie from my seat, telling her about the howl of mountain wind, like a freight train tearing through the dark, and the cold that clung to me. I'd passed the 500-mile mark, nearly a quarter of the trail, but I was tired of waking up in frozen clothes and boots. When the food arrived, piled high and steaming, I ended the call and dug in.

That night, with clean laundry from the motel machines and a gas station resupply in my pack, I felt ready to face whatever came next. I had hiked 43 miles in two days, over a week ahead of my original plan!

April 24, 2012 – Tuesday

Plus-Two and I started the day at The Barn again, with a big breakfast and hot coffee, no rush. With bellies full, we climbed back to the AT. The trail rolled up and down all day, testing our legs but not our spirits. Somewhere along the way, we ran into Gunrunner and Spock, the latter just returning after an injury had pulled him from the trail months before.

The air was crisp but kind, a far cry from yesterday's storm. Around one bend, we hit trail magic: coolers full of sandwiches, cookies, and cold soda.

I cracked open an orange pop and grinned like a kid. Plus-Two and I took photos for our families, trying to capture the joy of small, unexpected gifts.

We reached Knot Maul Branch Shelter on Lynn Camp Mountain, but it was already full. No matter. We pushed on to a spot by Lick Creek, set up camp, and cooked dinner. Plus-Two taught me a trick, pour boiling water straight into the food pouch instead of dirtying a cup. Less cleanup, more warmth in my hands.

We talked for a while before retreating to our tents.

April 25, 2012 – Wednesday

The rain returned in the night, so Plus-Two and I packed our things with our rain gear already on and began the climb up Chestnut Ridge. The ascent was unrelenting, an undulating rollercoaster of steep ups and downs.

We reached Chestnut Knob Shelter at 4,409 feet, grateful for its dry interior, and ate breakfast out of the weather. The rain stopped around 10 a.m., a small gift, and we peeled off the rain jackets, happy to feel the cool air on our shirts. But the trail had its own way of reminding me how quickly things could turn.

While crossing a large rock, my foot slipped. I twisted my left knee hard, the "good" one. My right knee had been through surgery before; now the other one was throbbing. There was no real option to stop and rest. On the Appalachian Trail, unless you want to run out of food or daylight, you keep walking. I managed just over 20 miles to Laurel Creek before calling it a day.

We pitched our tents early, laying gear out to dry and studying maps by the fading light. My knee worried me.

April 26, 2012 – Thursday

The rain showed no mercy. Still, I awoke with gratitude. My new single-person tent had kept me and my gear dry. We rolled up wet tents, started our morning hike, and soon came to a normally small creek now swollen into a six-foot-wide, knee-deep torrent. We stripped off boots and socks, rolled up pants, and stepped into icy water that made my legs ache with every step. It was just another reminder, on the trail, "comfort" is a word for a different life.

We saw no one all day. At Helvey's Mill Shelter, three hikers had taken over the space to play cards, gear blocking the entrance, unwilling to make room. That kind of selfishness was rare on the AT, but it stung in the cold rain. Plus-Two and I ate lunch on the edge of the shelter, then pushed on to Jenny Knob before dark.

Fidget and Mimi, a kind couple from Texas, welcomed us inside. They'd taken a Zero day to avoid the weather. Mimi snored loudly all night, and a few more hikers squeezed in later. Unlike the hikers at the previous shelter, most AT hikers are very friendly and thoughtful and always willing to squeeze in one more hiker, even in a crowded shelter.

April 27, 2012 – Friday

Plus-Two and I decided we made good trail partners, same pace, same early starts. At 6:40 a.m., we were climbing again. Cool air, no rain at last. The trail followed swollen Dismal Creek through pine forest, the kind of peaceful stretch that made me forget my aching knee for a while.

After lunch at Wapiti Shelter, we climbed to Doc's Knob over a rocky path that punished the feet. Twenty-two and a half miles later, I was exhausted. Two section hikers were there, both named Coach, both wrestling coaches from different states who had met years earlier and now hiked together. Their camaraderie was a reminder that the AT forges strong, lasting friendships.

Then the peace was shattered. Around dusk, hikers began arriving in thrift-store costumes, clearly drunk, explaining they were in the middle of a "24/24 Challenge" to complete 24 miles and 24 beers in 24 hours hiking in these crazy clothes. Spidderman (not Spiderman, he carefully explained) in a black raincoat, a man in a dress, someone in a leopard-print skirt, it was chaos. They came and went through the night, stumbling off into the dark. I couldn't imagine trying to walk the trail like that. Out here, I had a hard enough time just staying upright in the daytime, while sober!

April 28, 2012 – Saturday

We were up before 6 a.m. and cruised the eight downhill miles into Pearisburg, eager for a real bed and a hot meal. Timing mattered; I needed my resupply package from Stephanie before the post office closed at noon. Missing it would have cost me the whole weekend.

At the Plaza Motel, the owner did our laundry, one of those small kindnesses that mean the world to hikers.

We hit an all-you-can-eat Chinese buffet and made a dent in their reserves. I was discovering the "foolproof hiker diet" really was foolproof: eat anything, burn it all, still lose weight.

Later, with my gear restocked and organized, I sat with my feet up, updating Stephanie. My body was lean and hard again, like back in high school when I ran cross-country, but my knees were a different story. You can't really train for this; twenty miles a day, day after day, it wears you down in ways you only understand by living it.

Stephanie reminded me I could slow down, take rest days. But I couldn't shake the fear that something would stop me from finishing. Out here, failure felt like more than just quitting a hike; it felt like letting go of something I'd built my whole life toward.

So, I set a short-term goal: 730 miles by May 7. A third of the trail in a third of the time. One resupply to the next, one step to the next.

That evening, I was able to watch Buffalo Sabres hockey on TV. A lifelong fan, it was really rough to miss watching all the games, especially as they finally made the play-offs that year.

Plus-Two was kind enough to watch as well. It meant a slightly later night than usual, but the comfort of real beds meant we both slept well.

April 29, 2012 – Sunday

We were checked out of the motel by 7 a.m., grabbing a greasy breakfast from a fast-food joint on our way back to the trail. I even wrote in my journal that "the grease was free with your meal." Not my finest dining experience.

The AT wound through town for a while before we crossed a bridge over the New River, and then it went straight uphill. The trail was rocky, the kind of rocks the trail maintainers toss in to control erosion. I know it's necessary, but I hated it. The sharp edges pressed right through my boots, and more than once the stones rolled underfoot, threatening to twist my ankle. Over the course of Virginia, those rocks would leave me with most of the little injuries I'd collect, foot pain, sore joints, all from trudging over that unstable ground.

Virginia was different from the states before. I noticed the maintainers didn't seem to divert water off the trail, and with all the rain we'd had, it felt like I spent 80% of my time in wet, stinking boots.

We crossed the ridge running along the border between Virginia and West Virginia, a hard push, but eventually made it to Pine Swamp Branch Shelter after 19 miles with packs heavy from fresh food supplies. The first day out of town is always rough; your shoulders ache under the extra weight of all the packed food, and every climb feels twice as long.

The shelter itself was a nice surprise. More like a cabin than a lean-to, with bunks for sixteen and even a fireplace. A few hikers were there who had Zero'd in Pearisburg, just starting back out. One was a guy named Dutchman, someone I'd end up yo-yoing with for weeks. He'd hike fast and hard, then take long, lazy Zero days in town. One day, he'd fly past me, the next I'd pass him while he rested. Different rhythms, same destination.

I was bone-tired and irritated at myself for feeling so drained after a rest day. But Plus-Two's cheerful presence pulled me out of my funk. We joined the circle of conversation; trail conditions, gear, and the occasional mention of home. I admitted I was missing my family and missing Stephanie. Plus-Two had heard me say it before, but listened again, sharing in return about his kids and how excited he was to head home for his daughter's graduation. That camaraderie, the simple act of sharing a fire with other hikers, worked like medicine.

April 30, 2012 – Monday

The day started gently enough, the trail blessedly level for a short while. But soon the climbing began again, the ground littered with more rocks. My mood sank with each mile. I couldn't shake the exhaustion. Dark thoughts crept in. What if I just quit? Walked away from the whole thing? Maybe it was the place itself; we'd started the day crossing something called Dismal Branch, which seemed fitting.

We stopped for lunch at War Spur Shelter. The food and rest helped, but the real lift came a little later when we stumbled upon trail magic! There was a cooler tucked in the woods near Mountain Lake Road, filled with soda. Cold, sweet, and utterly unexpected. Strangers had hauled it there for no reason other than kindness, and that small act cracked my bad mood. Most hikers had been thoughtful enough to pack their empties back into the cooler; an extra step when so many are bone-weary.

We stopped after 18.5 miles at Laurel Creek Shelter, where the two section hikers known as Coach were camped. The older one launched into a string of stories about "Ragman," some fictional character he'd invented. The laughter around the shelter was easy and genuine. Nights like that made the miles worth it.

May 1, 2012 – Tuesday

The day started with a soaking. I slipped while crossing a creek and "turtled", flat on my back in the water, pack pinning me down. I couldn't get up without flailing like an overturned beetle. Plus-Two stood on the bank laughing so hard he could barely breathe. My pride was bruised, but nothing else. It's still one of those trail memories we laugh about years later.

We didn't hike together long that day, only about three miles to Route 42, where his parents picked him up for his daughter's college graduation. He promised to try and catch up when he came back Sunday. Watching him drive away left me oddly lonely, but also aware that this was part of the thru-hiker's life; people appear and disappear, sometimes for good, sometimes just long enough to make you appreciate their return.

I was alone again, but I pushed myself hard and finished over 22 miles of tough hiking. The day started with two big climbs. The first was up Sinking Creek Mountain, where I scrambled over boulders on the first ridge. The second, Brush Mountain, was even longer. At the top, I found an overgrown road and a stone memorial to Audie Murphy, near the spot where he died in a plane crash.

Past the memorial, the AT ran along a rocky ridge with a gorgeous view of the valley below. But the long descent that followed took more out of me than either climb; my knees have never liked downhills. The day ended with a mile-long climb to Pickle Branch Shelter. The access trail to the shelter added another half mile, frustrating because it didn't "count" toward my AT mileage, but my legs still felt every step.

I would have preferred to stop at a shelter closer to the AT, but I was too spent to push for the next one. No one else stayed there that night. For the first time on the trail, I was completely alone. I crawled into my sleeping bag at 7:30 p.m. with a book but gave up reading within minutes. By 8:00 p.m., I was asleep.

Chapter 4

Going Solo

Virginia

May 2, 2012 – Wednesday

Even after that early bedtime, I slept later than usual and didn't get moving until almost 8:00 a.m.. The trail was rocky and slow-going. Near Dragon's Tooth I had to climb down rock faces on hands and knees, my heavy pack making it even harder. Dragon's Tooth itself, a jagged stone pillar, was impressive, but I was too worn out to linger.

The descent was rough, and then the trail turned uphill again for most of the rest of the day. By the time I reached Catawba Mountain Shelter around 4:00 p.m., I was cooked. I drank a lot of water, knowing I still wasn't drinking enough. I hate stopping to find water, filter it, and treat it, so I tend to push through without enough water breaks.

That night I set up in the shelter, but by 11:00 p.m. I gave up trying to sleep. One section hiker's snores cut right through my earplugs. In the dark, I hauled myself out and pitched my tent nearby, not a great spot, but it was quieter.

May 3, 2012 – Thursday

McAfee Knob was only about an hour's hike from the shelter. I woke to the sound of hikers passing my tent at 4:30 a.m., heading for sunrise. I reached the Knob by 8:00 a.m., and the view was everything it's said to be. Spidderman, one of the Pearisburg Challenge hikers, happened by and snapped a photo of me standing on the rock ledge.

The adrenaline from reaching such a well-known AT landmark carried me quickly along Tinker Ridge. I did lose the trail briefly near Tinker Cliffs but found it again and made it to Lamberts Meadow Shelter for lunch. The Roanoke Valley stretched out below, dotted with farms, a peaceful scene.

Past the shelter, the ridge turned rocky again before dropping to Tinker Creek. I'd planned to camp there but found no decent sites, and the only water was swampy, possibly fouled by farm runoff. Hot and thirsty, I pushed on another half mile to Daleville, where I got a room at the Howard Johnson's.

The air-conditioned room felt like luxury. I offered to wash laundry for two younger hikers staying there, then sat naked in the cool air talking to Stephanie on the phone while my clothes tumbled in the dryer. I only carried two sets of clothes, and both were filthy and sweat-soaked. After a long shower, scrubbing twice, I felt human again.

Stephanie told me I sounded discouraged. She read me messages from friends and family, including my brother-in-law Steve, who said, "Greg is just too stubborn to quit." That made me laugh, because he's right. My grand-niece Audrey sent a sweet warning to watch out for bears. One message stuck with me all night, from a former section hiker named Singing Grizz: *"Pain is temporary, the memories are forever."*

May 4, 2012 – Friday

Breakfast at the hotel buffet was heaven; I had donuts, waffles, muffins, cereal, juice, coffee… a far cry from my usual two packets of instant oatmeal. I set out down the road afterward and promptly went the wrong way. The white blazes marking the AT aren't as frequent in Virginia, but my wrong turn worked out. I needed to get to Troutville anyway for a supply box from Jarrod and maps from Stephanie. Once I had them, I backtracked to rejoin the AT.

The trail followed the Blue Ridge Parkway, scenic, fairly level, and easy to make time on. I reached my original goal early enough to push on to Bobblets Gap Shelter, ending with 18.5 miles for the day and a light rain at the end. It was still an easy day compared to what I'd been through.

Stephanie noticed right away that I sounded like a different person than the night before, upbeat and positive. Rest, food, and an easier trail had done their magic. I told her I'd now hiked a full third of the AT, three days ahead of schedule.

We discussed resupply logistics. I was hiking much faster than expected, so the original plan needed adjusting. Jarrod had sent a bag of dehydrated chili, lighter, easier to prepare, more filling, and tastier than supermarket food. The six days' worth he sent should get me 100 miles to Montebello, where I could shop for my own supplies.

Poor planning out here could literally mean going hungry. Food and water are never far from a hiker's mind.

By nightfall, two more hikers arrived: Stray Dog, a friendly but eccentric young man, and Badger, an engineer who hikes exactly 16 miles a day, every day, no more and no less. He sleeps in a hammock strung between trees, no matter where that mileage leaves him. Out here, everyone has their own system.

May 5, 2012 – Saturday

Stray Dog's alarm jolted me awake, a harsh intrusion after weeks of waking to birdsong and the slow light of sunrise. The morning began gently enough, the trail kind to my legs, but by midday, I had my first blister on the small toe of my left foot. I told myself I'd stop and tape it, but the rain had already started, soaking everything, and I pushed on. That was a mistake. The blister split open, a sharp sting with every step, forcing me to stop anyway and fumble with the tape in the downpour. I limped to the next shelter just to patch it properly from my first aid kit, but even then, the pain stayed with me.

By the time I reached Bryant Ridge Shelter, I'd only managed 13.5 miles. Stray Dog and Badger arrived just as the rain began again, but both pushed on, Badger chasing his self-imposed 16-mile minimum. I stayed put. Tomorrow would bring the climb up Floyd Mountain, and I needed my foot in better shape for it.

The three-sided shelter itself was a marvel, two levels, well-built, enough room for a small army. No one else came that night, my second night truly alone on the trail. I pitched my tent inside to block the wind and rain. Sometime after midnight, I woke to the sound of animals growling and fighting nearby. My heart pounded as I pulled my trekking poles into the tent, just in case, but the noises drifted off into the dark. Sleep didn't come easily after that.

May 6, 2012 – Sunday

Alone or not, my morning rhythm was the same, and I was hiking by 7:15 a.m. Overcast skies kept the heat down, but most of the day was nothing but climbing, from 1,300 feet to 4,200, then back down, then up again. My toe throbbed, but yesterday's rest helped enough that I could hold a decent pace.

I caught Badger during lunch, then again later in the afternoon, and we hiked together for a bit before he stopped at his 16-mile mark. I went a mile further to Marble Spring, where I met a southbound (SOBO) couple from Cleveland. We talked until the light faded. Dinner was the freeze-dried chili Jarrod had sent. It was better than anything I'd eaten in weeks, rich and filling in a way the patchwork meals I'd been carrying simply weren't. Not all calories are created equal, and Jarrod knew it. I slept with a full stomach and the satisfaction that comes with it.

May 7, 2012 – Monday

Rain hammered the shelter roof all night, and I woke to a wet, misty morning. I decided to skip breakfast and make the five miles to the next shelter before eating. I caught Badger, but he kept going while I stopped to cook. We crossed the James River Foot Bridge together later that morning, though he fell behind again, worried about a sore knee from an earlier fall.

The trail followed the river, then climbed to a ridge that was supposed to hold some of the best views on the AT. I wouldn't know, fog and drizzle hid everything. Nine hours of head-down hiking in the wet brought me to Punch Bowl Shelter, where Badger also showed up.

I was the fifth hiker to claim a spot, but then Instigator and Expediter arrived, insisting on squeezing in. I'd met them before; she had a voice that grated like sandpaper, so I pitched my tent outside rather than listen to her. The spring peepers filled the dark with their endless chorus. However, I'll take frog noise over a snoring companion any day.

May 8, 2012 – Tuesday

I left at 7:15 a.m., Badger already ahead, but caught him soon enough. We made quick miles together, at one point, 2 miles in 40 minutes, which felt like flying on tired legs. We parted ways when I stopped for lunch before climbing Brown Mountain.

At Route 60, we found trail magic again! Candy bars and soda. Badger headed into Lexington with Lemmiwinks and Professor Oak, two young Virginia Tech hikers who could walk fast but couldn't seem to pack enough food. I kept climbing, a four-mile push over Bald Knob in steady rain, ending at Cow Camp Shelter after 15 miles.

Inside were Ace of Spades and Hummingbird, both pharmacy professors, plus a pharma sales rep, so half the evening's talk was about drugs of the legal variety.

Instigator and Expediter came in later, followed by a trail runner who updated us on conditions and warned of bad weather ahead, and the need to make room for extra bodies in the shelter. Motown, a young woman I'd met back near Pearisburg, showed up last. The rain pounded the tin roof, wind rattling the walls. We huddled in the dim light, each of us hoping the weather would break by morning.

May 9, 2012 – Wednesday

Mist and fog clung to the mountains after another wet night. At this point, I'd almost forgotten what it felt like to be dry. The trail gave me a couple of climbs in the morning, but nothing too difficult. What really slowed me down was the blister on my left little toe, it refused to heal. It threw off my balance just enough to keep me irritated all day. On top of that, the constant pounding of my toenails against my boots had left bruises under several of them, and my skin was breaking down from wearing wet socks and boots for days.

By the time I reached The Priest Shelter, 8 hours and 16.8 miles later, heavy rain had set in again. The place was already full: Lemmiwinks and Professor Oak, a new face named J.D., plus Motown, Expediter, and Instigator. Those last two had been shadowing my pace for days, and I still found them grating. As I listened to their chatter, I quietly made a plan; tomorrow, I'd out-hike them for good. Motown, Lemmiwinks, and Professor Oak were all planning a longer 22-mile day. That became my goal, too.

May 10, 2012 – Thursday

Today was my grandson Riley's second birthday. Back in Buffalo, my family would be gathering for a party. Both my sons have birthdays coming up this month, too, all of which I'd miss. Family weighed heavy on my mind, and for the first time in a while, I felt real homesickness.

The morning was cool and clear, a relief after five straight days of rain. Virginia's slogan is "Virginia is for lovers," but I'd been finishing that sentence in my head with "…but I don't love Virginia." Today, though, I began to see its charm. From the summit of The Priest, the views opened up, the Blue Ridge stretching away under a cloudless sky.

The day was long, 12 hours, 22 miles, and much of it was on a rocky trail that punished my sore feet. But when I reached Humpback Mountain Overlook, the reward was worth every step: a sweeping panoramic view and a sunset that lit the mountains in gold and fire. This was the kind of moment I'd imagined when I first dreamed of hiking the AT.

Lemmiwinks, Professor Oak, and Motown arrived an hour later but decided to push on. I stayed. The site had no shelter, no privy, just views. As night fell, I realized I'd have the mountaintop to myself. The air turned cold, but I slept well. At one point, I woke to a crystal-clear sky filled with stars and the distant glow of town lights. With no one to disturb, I wandered around quietly in the dark, soaking it all in.

May 11, 2012 – Friday

The morning air up on the mountain was bitter, so I packed quickly. The trail crossed more rocky sections of Humpback Mountain, then eased into a long downhill. I stopped at the first shelter for breakfast, then pushed on to Rockfish Gap. By just afternoon, I'd hiked 12 miles, a pace that amazed me compared to my first weeks on the trail, when 8 or 10 miles in a whole day left me exhausted. I felt a quiet pride in how far I'd come.

At Rockfish Gap, I called a number posted near the road and got a ride from a man named Roy into Waynesboro. My plan had been to meet Stephanie here in a day or two, but my fast pace to shake Instigator and Expediter had landed me in town early. My mail package hadn't arrived yet, and the post office was officially closed on Saturday, but the clerk told me to come around to the back the next day and he'd hand it to me.

Jarrod had arranged for me to stay with Karen and Bill, parents of his Army buddy Lee. Though we'd never met, our sons had served together in Iraq, and that was enough. When I called Karen, she said she could pick me up after teaching her afternoon class. She drove me to their house, gave me a tour, and then handed me keys to both the house and a car. They were leaving for a family wedding and were literally turning their home over to a stranger. She pointed to the stocked fridge and told me to eat whatever I liked. Their trust and generosity floored me.

Bill arrived shortly after, then whisked Karen off for their weekend away. Alone in the house, I did laundry, took a long shower, and then drove to the store to buy supplies for the next six days on the trail. Back at the house, I called Stephanie and cracked my first beer in a month, a Czech Pilsner that tasted impossibly good. As I sipped it, I noticed a few small handyman jobs that needed doing, so I found some tools in the basement and fixed them. It seemed the least I could do for such kindness.

May 12, 2012 – Saturday (Zero)

I woke at my usual early hour, the kind of morning where the light slips in just enough to stir me. Karen had pointed out the farm-fresh eggs in the fridge, so I scrambled up a hearty breakfast before heading out. Driving their Volvo into Waynesboro felt almost strange, rolling along on smooth pavement instead of pounding my feet against the rocky AT.

First stop was the post office to pick up the map package Stephanie had sent Priority Mail to reach me at my faster pace. With that in hand, I headed to the outfitter for much-needed replacements: my food bag and clothes bag had both ripped, casualties of too many wet, rough days. My pack is my little ecosystem, everything has a place, and I can find it even in the dark, but that only works if my gear is intact. I picked up a new tent footprint, stove fuel, and batteries for my water purifier, then drove back to the house just before noon.

And wouldn't you know it, when I'm not hiking, the day is flawless. Clear, sunny, perfect. What is it about me that summons rain the moment my boots hit the trail? Maybe my trail name should've been *Rain Bringer*.

I walked to Coffee on the Corner for a Reuben and a glass of porter, meeting Karen and Bill's daughter Clare there. Back at the house, I sorted and packed my new supplies, then decided to straighten up the basement as a small thank-you. I noticed the back door handle was broken, so I hopped in the car for a quick run to the hardware store, grabbed some screws, and fixed it. Dinner was Subway, as I didn't feel right eating *all* of Karen and Bill's food, even though they'd offered. Not that I hadn't been grazing on their snacks all day.

In the evening, I called Larissa, then Colleen, then Stephanie. She was surprised at my pace, happy I was taking a break, and excited about seeing me next week. It would be six weeks since Easter, the longest we'd been apart since we met three years ago.

She asked what it was like hiking solo, what I thought about all day. I told her that mostly, I'm focused on my feet, because one wrong step could mean the end of the hike. I keep an eye out for snakes, too. No more venomous ones lately, just big black rat snakes. I make a goal each morning and think about that, the miles, my pace, where I'll camp. And then I admitted it: I'm terribly homesick. I miss my family. I miss her. I even miss the people from work I thought I'd left behind without a second glance.

Still, there's comfort in the rhythm of the trail: walk, set camp, write, sleep, repeat. I've also learned to value water in a way I never imagined. When you have to find and purify every drop you drink, it becomes the center of your day. Lately, even more so.

By the time I hung up, I felt lighter. Fed, rested, and content, I ended the day watching hockey, then sinking into the best night's sleep I'd had in weeks.

May 13, 2012 – Sunday

Another good breakfast, another small fix, tidying up the area by the back door where I'd replaced the handle. It was Mother's Day, but also Premiere League soccer day, so I watched a match until Karen and Bill returned around noon. We talked for a bit before they packed me into their car and drove me back to Rockfish Gap. I said my many thank-yous for their generosity, shouldered my pack, and stepped back into the woods.

Less than a mile in, I was at the Shenandoah National Park boundary, filling out a self-registration form for my camping permit. Choices for camping were slim, so I took the first available spot, Calf Mountain Shelter, just seven miles from Rockfish Gap, deep in the trees.

My two days off meant a whole new cast of shelter-mates: Rook, a friendly young woman; Dundee, a tall Australian on his third pair of shoes; Daypack, a veteran AT hiker; and two others, Stinger and No Sweat. A full house of strangers.

And, right on cue, the rain came in the evening. Of course it did. Maybe *Rain Bringer* really is my trail name.

May 14, 2012 – Monday

The day dawned as what I now called a typical Virginia day—rain, fog, and miserable. The trail wasn't difficult, but the rain made it wet and slippery. I just put my head down so the rain dripped off my hat and walked for just over 20 miles. Nothing to see but wet woods. Everyone from the night before met up at the same shelter for lunch, getting out of the rain to eat. Spec, a University of Virginia student, came by saying he was conducting a study about the mental state of thru-hikers, and asked us all to complete a survey. It was probably not a good day to collect that data, but we all answered willingly.

I camped at the side of the AT on Loft Mountain. I set up my tent in the rain and had to cook dinner inside. I preferred cooking outside, since the fuel included an open flame, but I just wasn't going to sit in the rain. Rook, the young woman I had met the night before, was camped nearby and told me she was going to spend 12 straight hours in her sleeping bag just to warm up. I noticed that she had set up her tent in a bad spot down the trail. Feeling paternal and protective, I told her of a better spot a little farther up, so she moved. We spoke briefly, and I found out that she was going to med school, but then we retreated to our respective tents. She really did stay in her tent for 12 straight hours.

The rain slowed but never stopped. It turned out we were only about half a mile from an official campground, but neither of us realized it at the time. Setting up a tent by the side of the trail was called "stealth camping," frowned upon but not against the rules. I had just stopped there because I was too wet and miserable to go further. However, I usually tried to make it to a shelter or campground for the advantage of having a privy, if nothing else. Although one could obviously relieve oneself in the woods, digging a hole to squat and then bury was a pain, so I made sure to take advantage of the privies, and I was quite appreciative of that amenity.

May 15, 2012 – Tuesday

The rain had kept up until 4 a.m., and I hadn't slept well but still got up at my normal time. The day started gloomy, but the weather improved a bit in the morning. I made it to Pinefield Hut, where I snacked a bit and then pushed on. There were a lot of hills, and I found myself losing all my energy. I needed to eat, but the rain started again, and everything was wet, so I just kept moving. I ended up at Hightop Hut after only 14 miles. I had wanted to cover more mileage that day, but the rain turned heavy, and I decided to stop for the night. I was depressed and discouraged by the constant rain.

Then a small group of hikers came in, and everything changed. A small woman named Mouse (her real name was "Mickey," thus the humorous trail name), an older man named Blue (the second Blue I'd met), and a 30-something named Steve-O arrived and seemed to bring happiness with them. They had been hiking together for a while and were a positive and friendly bunch. Spec, the student with the thru-hiker survey, came in as well, and the conversation turned lively.

They challenged me to keep up with them the next day. They were planning to hike 23.9 miles, which would be more than I had ever hiked in one day. They were so much fun and so encouraging that I agreed to the goal. It was going to be a long day.

May 16, 2012 – Wednesday

I started out early, knowing that I hiked best in the morning and needed to push myself to make the goal. The trail was up and down but fairly easy. I got to Lewis Mountain Campground at lunchtime and was able to purchase some food there that was a lot better than the trail mix I usually munched on at noon. Fueled with the good meal, I worked really hard to make it to Rock Spring Cabin and meet the crew of my new hiker friends. Luckily, the hike was fairly easy, paralleling the highway through Shenandoah National Park. Unfortunately, the trail was below the highway and missed all the vistas that car travelers enjoyed. Still, it was a pretty walk.

Along the way, I saw Rook with her parents, who had joined her for this stretch of the trail. It was her last day on the AT as she was returning to the "real world" for graduation. She was a little thing with a steely determination, and I was sure that whatever she ended up doing, she would undoubtedly succeed. She could certainly out-hike me!

I joined the others at the Big Meadow Wayside, a restaurant in the park, and was overwhelmed as they all congratulated me on hiking my longest day ever. We enjoyed a three-piece chicken dinner and a blackberry shake. Steve-O surprised us by purchasing beer and wine to share. He told us this was to celebrate completing 900 miles on the AT, a milestone we had passed that day. We walked to the shelter and finished the night roasting marshmallows, munching cookies, and drinking beer. I realized that this type of camaraderie was what I had been missing by hiking alone.

May 17, 2012 – Thursday

My new comrades had a plan to hike 28 miles for the day. They insisted I would do the same, laughing and refusing to listen to my concerns. This was double the average mileage I had been hiking on the AT. Even hiking flat trails at home, I had never hiked that far in one day. Admittedly, the trail was well-groomed and rolling rather than rocky and mountainous. Also, there were restaurants along the way so we could fuel up. Even so, it was going to be a long, long day.

I started a little before 7 a.m., munching on two Uglies (massive, 2000-calorie donuts) that I had purchased at the store the night before. After a four-mile hike together, Steve-O, Blue, Mouse, and I stopped for breakfast at the Skyline Restaurant. For this "second breakfast," I piled in eggs, sausage, hash browns, biscuits and gravy, and washed it down with coffee. "A good way to start," I reflected. Blue generously settled the tab for the whole group.

We continued along fairly close together, with Mouse providing constant encouragement for me: "You can do it, you've got this!" After 21 miles of hiking, Mouse, Blue, and I stopped at Elk Wallow for a cheeseburger and a shake. And there were still seven more miles to go. My pace was slower now, and the others went on ahead, but told me that I WOULD join them that evening, no excuses allowed. "You will be there!" was the last thing Mouse said before turning to hike ahead.

The trail continued steady and straight, with no big mountains. I arrived to join the group at Gravel Springs Hut to their cheers after 13 hours of hiking. It was getting dark, and it seemed like there were people everywhere. I would never have been able to make that distance if the trail had not been relatively easy, and restaurant food not available to fuel my body. Additionally, the encouragement of the others pulled me on beyond what I would have done on my own. It was odd how quickly friendship could develop with this type of shared experience.

I ate more dinner before settling into my sleeping bag, exhausted, only to find that my legs ached so badly I couldn't get to sleep for quite a while. This would be my longest daily distance hiked for my entire AT journey. *An unforgettable day.*

May 18, 2012 – Friday

We all got up in the morning and said our good-byes. Mouse and Blue were going to meet their respective spouses for the weekend. Steve-O was going to rest and resupply at Front Royal. That was the town where Stephanie had planned to meet me, but my fast pace the past two days completely shot those plans down. I didn't want to take time off in town to wait for her to arrive the next day, so I would be hiking on. Exchanging contact info (including "real world" names), my new friends all went their separate ways.

I hiked out of the park and down to Route 522, an easy and fast hike. After that, it was a long uphill, which took a lot out of me. My legs hadn't really recovered from the previous day's marathon hike. However, once up the hill, the trail became easier.

The weather stayed good, so I was able to make good time and arrived at Jim and Molly Denton Shelter for the night. There was a shower available, which was appreciated but very cold. My head and feet enjoyed a cold wash after the hot day of hiking, however.

Two section hikers, Kim and Kate from nearby Virginia Tech, were also at the shelter. They were going to hike through the Shenandoahs as a trial run to see if they would want to hike the entire AT. I offered my maps, since I had now hiked beyond them, so they were just extra weight, chatted a bit about the trail, and gave them some ideas for their hike. I called Stephanie to let her know that I was already past our planned rendezvous spot at Front Royal and she exclaimed, "You must have grown wings on your feet!" She was leaving Buffalo the next day, hoping to make the drive to meet me all in one day. We planned a few possible rendezvous spots for the next evening as I reviewed my map, and she verified that her phone map had the AT programmed in.

May 19, 2012 – Saturday

I woke up excited and early—Stephanie was driving down to Virginia from Buffalo today and would meet me tonight! I started off with a climb but hardly noticed it. The trail seemed to just flow easily all day as I focused on seeing her soon. I got a cell signal at Ashby Gap and called her to verify that she would be able to make the entire drive in one day. She wasn't quite as far along as I had hoped, so I looked at the map and decided to make it a 22-mile day and meet her a little further along the AT than we had planned, at Route 605.

The trail was good until I reached a stretch called the Roller Coaster. This section had a lot of small hills, and the trail was poorly maintained, making for a difficult end to my day. I arrived at the rendezvous spot, a gravel road in the woods at 5:05 p.m., exhausted and thirsty.

After waiting 5 minutes, I decided to call Stephanie to see how far away she was. She answered on her car Bluetooth, saying, "Do you see a cloud of dust up the hill to your right?" I looked and saw a car coming down the road toward me. "That's me!" she exclaimed.

Stephanie had left Buffalo early that Saturday morning. It was about 430 miles to the section of Virginia where I was hiking, and that would push her limits for driving alone in one day. We had discussed the possibility of her taking two days to arrive and meeting me Sunday, but after six weeks, the longest we had ever been apart in the three years we'd been dating, we both hoped she could make the trip in one day.

When I first called, she was in Pennsylvania, not as far along as we'd hoped, so we worked out an alternative rendezvous spot a little further up the AT. She knew that meant I'd have a really long day of hiking. Thinking of how hot the day was, and knowing hikers are always hungry, she picked up a large Subway sandwich and a gallon of Gatorade at her lunch stop and packed them in a cooler to surprise me.

She managed the entire drive, reaching close to the rendezvous spot shortly after 5 p.m. with only a couple of missed turns. She had assumed Route 605 would be paved and completely ignored the gravel roads crossing the highway, having to backtrack when she realized she'd missed the turn. Route 605 turned out to be a 1.5-lane gravel road up a hill in the woods, not too well-maintained. She stopped at the top of a steep hill to check her map and change out of sweaty travel clothes into a nice dress, fixing her hair like we were going on a date. It had been a long six weeks, and she wanted to look her best. When I called, she got back in the car and started down the steep hill in a cloud of dust I could see. We had started our day 430 miles apart and ended up at the rendezvous spot only 5 minutes apart. Later, Stephanie realized that if she hadn't stopped to dress up, we probably would have arrived at exactly the same moment!

The car reached the spot where I was waiting as Route 605 crossed the AT. Stephanie was out almost before it stopped, and we clung to each other in a long hug. She noticed I had lost a lot more weight since she'd last seen me at Easter, with my clothes hanging on me. I was happy to see her, but exhausted. She had the gallon of Gatorade in her hand, and I quickly grabbed it and drank half in one gulp. "I am so happy to see you!" I said. Then I added jokingly, "The only thing that would make this moment better would be a Subway sandwich!" She popped the trunk, opened the cooler, and—like Mary Poppins—magically pulled out exactly what I'd wished for: a foot-long sub sandwich absolutely loaded with all the veggies and meats possible. The look on my face must have been priceless as I grabbed it.

We tossed my pack into the trunk, and I fell into the passenger seat, devouring the sandwich and emptying the Gatorade within about two minutes. My happiness was complete when she showed me a bag of chocolate chip cookies baked by my daughter Larissa, and six of them were gone by the time we arrived at the Red Roof Inn she'd booked in Winchester, VA.

The motel was only 12 miles away, but the state of the roads made it a 30-minute drive. Even after getting onto paved roads, it was a mountainous, winding roller coaster of a drive.

Stephanie began to have some idea of what I'd hiked through that day. Once at the hotel, I began to clean up, and she could really see how emaciated I was. She was worried, but I laughed, saying I felt in the best shape I'd been in since high school. We discovered I had lost 30 pounds since starting the AT two months ago!

During my shower, I felt something just beyond my reach. Calling Stephanie, she found a tick on me and got it off. It had just started to attach, but didn't appear to have been feeding. Its size and patterned back meant it was a wood tick rather than the tiny, dark deer tick known to carry Lyme disease, which was a relief.

After the shower and a short rest, I was hungry again. Stephanie took me to a nearby steakhouse. Only 90 minutes after eating the foot-long and cookies, I consumed a bowl of soup, salad, steak, loaded potato, and bread, washing it down with a beer. My appetite finally calmed down, but that didn't stop me from grabbing a few more of Larissa's cookies back at the hotel. Stephanie told me her goal over the next couple of weeks together was to fatten me back up again!

That night, she tended to my feet, which were in bad shape with the blister now infected. Soaking my feet in Epsom salts and massaging in some healing oils helped the pain a bit. She was shocked at my exhaustion. Mouse had given me an energy supplement, which helped me make the huge mileage days, but apparently, it took a huge toll on me. Jarrod and Colleen called to say they were planning to drive out the next day from near Washington, D.C., where they lived. That gave me the excuse I needed to plan for a Zero day, and I went to sleep relaxed, full, and happy.

Chapter 5

Slack Packing

Virginia / West Virginia / Maryland / Pennsylvania

May 20, 2012 – Sunday (Zero)

My habit of early morning waking held true even though there was no need to get up. I ate breakfast at the motel with Stephanie, and Jarrod and Colleen arrived about 10:00 a.m. with some more hiker food packages and homemade white chocolate cupcakes. We caught up for a while, then Jarrod treated us all to lunch at Ruby Tuesday. He was also trying to get good nutrition into me and knew there was a salad buffet and plentiful food at that restaurant.

Back at the motel, I shared some pictures I'd been able to download from my camera to Stephanie's laptop. I showed her a picture of Blue, Mouse, and Steve-O and told the stories of my wonderful few days hiking with them. Other shots were of the scenery, but I admitted the pictures just didn't do it justice — you had to be there to truly experience the beauty. By then, I was hungry again, so we all went out for ice cream. (Calories in ice cream are a constant hiker's craving, and I was thrilled to enjoy a heaping cone.)

Jarrod and Colleen had to leave in the late afternoon for their drive back home, so Stephanie and I were alone again. I told her it was wonderful to see someone other than a hiker, and especially Jarrod and Colleen, who lived furthest from Buffalo of all my children. Food still being of critical importance, we went out for dinner at a Mexican restaurant nearby, then Stephanie spent more time working on my feet. At my request, she had brought my favorite low-topped hiking boots from Buffalo to replace the beat-up high-topped boots I had been wearing. We discovered that my feet had swollen and flattened so much from hiking that my old boots were now much too tight.

My blistered toe was responding to the treatment — and the relief of wearing sandals all day instead of boots — but it still hurt a lot. We finished the evening with Stephanie buzzing off the hair that had regrown since starting my hike a little over two months ago.

May 21, 2012 – Monday

Early the next morning, Stephanie watched as I became Hoot. I don't think she realized until that moment that there truly was a difference. To her, I had been Greg, her boyfriend, and Jarrod's dad. Now she saw the focused hiker, Hoot, preparing his pack and gear with single-mindedness for the day's hike.

One difference from before was that she would hold onto my main pack, while I carried only a small daypack with food, water, and essentials. In AT parlance, I was now "slack-packing," with the luxury of having a trail angel (Stephanie) collecting me off the trail each day so I didn't have to carry the full pack. We both hoped that a couple of weeks of slack-packing while she was with me would help me regain my health and strength. She planned to make sure I got good breakfasts and dinners, and would find motels along the trail so I wouldn't have to camp for the ten days we had together. This section of the AT was close to civilization, so we could plan to meet each night where the trail crossed local roads. She looked forward to her own kind of "vacation" spent doing computer work during the day, finding the next places to sleep and eat, and having her own small adventure, and we both looked forward to being together each night.

Because of our early wake-up, even with breakfast and the half-hour drive back to Route 605, I was back on the AT by 7:15 a.m. It was raining when we left the hotel, but pouring by the time we reached the trail. Or, as I said, "typical Virginia." I pulled on my gaiters, poncho, and the brimmed "Indiana Jones" hat I'd asked her to bring from Buffalo, and disappeared into the woods to tackle the rest of the Roller Coaster. My goal was Harpers Ferry, WV, a 25-mile hike. With slack-packing and a day of rest behind me, I hoped it would be easy. Up until now, all my AT hiking had been with a full pack, so I felt delightfully unencumbered. We had two alternative rendezvous spots picked out just in case.

I did fine for about 18 miles, but still had 7 to go when I reached Keys Gap. The wet trail along the VA/WV line was awful. There was no recent maintenance, and rocks were everywhere. Frustration hit hard. I even started chucking some of the rocks into the woods, swearing loudly.

By the time I finally reached Harpers Ferry, my bad mood hadn't improved, and then I learned Stephanie had changed our plans.

While I'd been hiking, she had scouted each alternate rendezvous spot, then decided to explore the Appalachian Trail Conservancy (ATC) near our original meeting place. It's the honorary halfway point of the AT (not exact, but over 1,000 miles from Springer Mountain) and a major psychological milestone for thru-hikers. Every thru-hiker stops here for a photo that goes in that year's hiker yearbook, along with their name, trail name, hometown, start date, and the date the picture was taken. The ATC also keeps the completed shelter logbooks where hikers sign in and leave messages.

When Stephanie walked in, she recognized two men from my photos, though she wasn't sure at first. An ATC employee mentioned "Steve-O," and she went right up to a young man she'd never met and asked, "Are you Steve-O?" His surprised "yesss?" was followed by a big smile when she said, "I'm Hoot's girlfriend." That was all it took. "You must be Stephanie!" he exclaimed, and she joined the little group. The other man was Blue, who was waiting for his wife, Debbie, to arrive. Debbie showed up around noon, and the four of them went out to lunch, talking and laughing like old friends.

Stephanie arranged to meet them all for dinner after I arrived, then found us lodging, the Harpers Ferry Hostel across the river in Maryland. It was cheap, which was important since we'd be paying for lodging during her whole stay.

When I reached the bridge over the Potomac around 6:30 p.m., I was mud-covered, hungry, drenched, and still angry at the trail. I wanted a clean hotel and a quiet evening with Stephanie. Instead, she told me we were going to meet my friends at a local all-you-can-eat Chinese Jumbo Buffet. My bad mood evaporated when I saw them. Debbie and Stephanie got to see how much hikers can eat, and everyone teased me mercilessly for slack-packing. We sat for hours swapping trail stories, laughing hard, and savoring the camaraderie.

Back at the hostel, though, we discovered our room was airless and hot, the bed lumpy, and there were stink bugs everywhere. Some dropped from the light fixture onto the bed! We kept our belongings in the car to avoid bringing any home with us. I slept just fine, though, even through a fierce thunderstorm. Compared to camping, it felt like luxury.

May 22, 2012 – Tuesday

I was happy to get up and leave the hostel that morning. Harpers Ferry is where Virginia, West Virginia, and Maryland all meet. The ATC is in WV, the hostel in MD, and I had hiked through VA to get there. A quick walk could cover three states! My first stop was breakfast at the Mountain View Diner in Charles Town, WV, where I had the best grits I've ever eaten. Then I swung by a local grocery store to pick up some trail food for my lunches while I waited for the ATC to open at 9:00 a.m.

Once it opened, I rummaged through the hiker box and scored a fuel canister for my stove, a headlamp, and a new hat, since my "Indiana Jones" hat unfortunately turned out to be useless in the rain. Hiker boxes are a staple along the AT at larger hostels, hotels, or gathering points like the ATC; places where hikers can leave gear they don't need and pick up something they do. One person's trash really is another person's treasure. Because I usually camped instead of staying at hostels, I hadn't seen many hiker boxes, so this one felt like a gold mine. I saw everything from soup packets to clothing, tea bags, power cords, and random gear.

There was a scale at the ATC, and I was pleased to see I'd gained back five pounds in the few days since Stephanie had arrived. Then came my official ATC hiker photo. I logged in as Hiker #181, and when I started at Amicalola Falls in Georgia I was #199, so it was clear some folks had already dropped out. Most hikers signing in had started around late March, weeks after me, but my slower pace and early breaks meant they'd already caught up. I insisted that Stephanie be in the picture because there's no way I'd have been able to hike the AT without her support.

Afterward, I went to an outfitter. I'd lost so much weight that my original pack was far too big. I loved it, but it just didn't fit anymore. I found a smaller, lighter pack I'd use once Stephanie left and my slack-packing "vacation" was over. Gear that works for *you* is critical on the trail; I'd heard countless shelter conversations about boots, sticks, and packs. My old "Gregory" pack (I loved the brand name!) would later go to my son Jarrod, who's taller and could use it.

By late morning, Stephanie dropped me at the parking lot by the Potomac bridge. I tested the new pack and it fit everything, though for that day's hike I'd only be using my simple daypack. I'm meticulous about packing. Rain gear, phone, and first aid go on top or in pockets. Camp-only items, like my sleeping roll, go at the bottom. Clothes and food are packed in water-resistant nylon bags. My fully loaded new smaller pack would be 30–35 pounds, depending on food and water.

With only the daypack on, I headed out. The trail took me through Harpers Ferry, across the Potomac, and onto the C&O Canal Towpath. I caught up with Steve-O for a few easy miles before he pulled ahead. I wouldn't see him again in person, though we stayed in touch. He went on to become an actor, popping up in commercials and TV shows.

It was a gorgeous day, and I was making great time. By mid-afternoon, I texted Stephanie to pick me up at Turners Gap, the farthest of the rendezvous points we'd planned. The last stretch was rocky, but I still arrived around 6:20 p.m. After dinner at Bob Evans, we stayed at a Super 8 hotel (no more hostels). I'd covered 18.4 miles in about 6.5 hours, almost 3 mph for my best pace yet. "Slack-packing is great!" I wrote in my journal.

May 23, 2012 – Wednesday

Stephanie dropped me back at Turners Gap around 8:45 a.m., later than usual after a leisurely breakfast. The first part of the hike flew by. I reached the I-71 footbridge about five hours later without seeing another hiker, though I did meet a ridge runner. A rocky section and a half-mile boulder field slowed me briefly, but with my daypack and a good night's sleep, it was nothing compared to carrying a full load.

By the time I reached Rte. 491 at Raven Rock Hollow, the sky looked ominous. I called Stephanie for a pickup after covering 17 miles, but in the 20 minutes it took her to arrive, the skies opened and there was thunder, lightning, and pouring rain. The hat I'd grabbed from the hiker box turned out to be as useless in the rain as my last one. Now I knew why someone had ditched it.

That night, back at the Super 8, we went to Texas Roadhouse for dinner. A foot rub afterward put me right to sleep.

May 24, 2012 – Thursday

I started early, hitting the trail before 7:30 a.m. The rocky terrain led me to the Mason-Dixon Line at the PA–MD border; my 7th state after GA, NC, TN, VA, WV, and MD. Crossing into Pennsylvania gave me a boost.

Stephanie texted to suggest a Zero day so we could explore Gettysburg together tomorrow. I decided to push for a long day to "earn" it. The rocky ridges eventually gave way to Rte. 30 in Caledonia State Park, and I reached it just as Stephanie drove up. I'd covered almost 24 miles, which, for me, was enough to take tomorrow off without guilt.

That evening, we checked into the Blue Sky Motel, had dinner at the Appalachian Brewing Company, and enjoyed a couple of craft beers. The food was disappointing, but it felt like date night. We took a quick drive through Gettysburg, saving the full tour for the next day, it would be a break for both of us.

May 25, 2012 – Friday (Zero)

It was a beautiful day for our planned trip to Gettysburg, as typical for any day I took a Zero (why did it always seem to rain when I hiked and be sunny when I took a Zero?). We got up early and went to Perkins for a good breakfast before driving out to Gettysburg past battlefields and then to the Visitor Center and Museum. First, we watched a movie, then visited the Cyclorama. Created in the 1880s, the Cyclorama is a huge (377 feet long and 42 feet high) hand-painted, detailed rendering of Pickett's Charge that circles 360 degrees around the viewer in a circular room, giving the impression of being on the battlefield no matter which direction you look. We finished with a slow walk through the museum displays. The information about the Civil War and the Battle at Gettysburg was well-presented and a sobering reminder of the horrors of war, especially a war pitting families and neighbors against each other over passionately held ideals and beliefs that could not be resolved any other way. We were somber as we left.

We spent the rest of the day relaxing, with lunch at a Thai restaurant and dinner at an Italian restaurant and enjoying time together

May 26, 2012 – Saturday

With the rest from the Zero day and the slack-packing, I felt I could make a 20-mile plan for my hike through Michaux State Forest, ending at Pine Grove Furnace State Park. Stephanie took me to Perkins for a good breakfast, so I felt great. The terrain was easier than usual, with few hills, and I was able to keep a 3 mph pace for a good portion of the day (my typical pace with a full pack was closer to 2 mph). I ran into Veggie Greens and Keeps Going, and we yo-yoed through the day. There were a lot of section and weekend hikers on this hike since it was the start of the Memorial Day weekend.

Partway through the day, I got trail magic from a former (2004) AT hiker and current trail maintainer and his wife, who supplied Gatorade and goodies for the hikers. I complained about the rocks on the trail and was told that it was intentional to prevent the trail from being worn away.

When I said that all it did was encourage hikers to go around the rock-covered spots, the maintainer was quite upset: "that makes it worse!" Unfortunately, hikers hated the rocks, which had sharp edges felt even through good hiking boots, but the foot traffic and weather wore away the trail continually. Trail maintenance was a thorny topic of discussion with hikers.

When I was a couple of miles from the rendezvous spot, I called Stephanie to let her know and discovered she was already waiting for me at the park. Just before reaching the park, I passed the Halfway Marker and snapped a selfie with a huge grin. I arrived just as the AT Museum located at the park was closing, but they slipped us in for a quick tour because I was a thru-hiker. When we left the museum, Veggie Greens and Keeps Going were sitting outside for a rest, so I was able to introduce Stephanie and chat a bit. Then Stephanie took me to the town of Carlisle where she had managed to get a good deal for a two-day stay at the Rodeway Inn. I cleaned up and grabbed a quick nap before we got dinner at a local place. I could certainly get used to daily slack-packing with good food, hotel beds, and Stephanie's company! Unfortunately, we only had a few more days together, so I resolved to enjoy every minute.

May 27, 2012 – Sunday

After breakfast at the same local restaurant, Stephanie drove me back to Pine Grove Furnace State Park. Then, she surprised me by walking alongside me for about a half-hour, until the trail turned out of the park to go uphill. The first 10 minutes of the trail were on a wide, flat bike path, and she teased me that this was like all the AT and I was faking it when I told her how hard the trail was. I slowed my pace while we were together, but it was still a very fast pace for her.

When the AT turned up the mountain and left the nice path, I called it a slight incline, but she was soon huffing and puffing like a steam engine. Despite her earlier teasing, she had great respect for me and all the AT hikers for taking on the physical challenge of the AT. She turned back with a wave after about a mile as I climbed on up the rougher trail.

After the initial climb, the trail flattened out for a while until, after crossing Rte. 94, there were some more climbs, including one fairly steep one. This was followed by a flat stretch across farm fields to Boiling Springs. The easy terrain tempted me to push beyond the planned rendezvous spot for a 23-mile day. It should have been easy, but I found myself completely out of energy.

I called Stephanie when I arrived at Rte. 641 and asked her to come collect me. She got there 10 minutes later, worried.

It was an extremely hot day, and Stephanie thought maybe I had heat exhaustion, since the open fields didn't have the protection from the sun like in the forest. I had actually hiked the day in some shorts that Stephanie had brought rather than my usual hiking pants, but I still complained of being too hot. I certainly felt hot to the touch, and I complained of feeling sick and being exhausted. My illness would take on significance in retrospect, but at the time we both just felt I needed rest and fluids.

May 28, 2012 – Monday

I still felt unusually tired, but figured that with a good breakfast and slack-packing, I could probably do OK. I cruised along the first 9 miles of fairly flat trail, making good time. However, at the first uphill, Blue Mountain, my energy completely dissipated. I stopped at the Darlington Shelter to eat lunch and call Stephanie. We arranged an early afternoon rendezvous at Rte. 850. Seeing me looking ill, Stephanie wanted me to stop and rest, and push fluids after hiking 12.5 miles in the 90-degree heat. She took me to the hotel for a nap, and I complained of feeling dizzy. Except for dinner at a local restaurant, I didn't leave my bed for the rest of the day.

May 29, 2012 – Tuesday (Zero)

I got up that morning and took stock of how I felt … tired, dizzy, and just "off." My body told me to stay put, and so did Stephanie. I hated the thought of losing precious time, but something wasn't right. I decided to take a Zero.

After a restful morning with a good breakfast and lots of fluids, I started to feel a little better around noon. We decided to go out shopping. My hiking boots had carried me 1,100 miles, but the rocky terrain had chewed the tread down to almost nothing. I've always preferred Merrells, so we went to the local dealer, but they didn't have the mid-height boots I wanted. The real surprise came when they measured my feet, which were a whole size bigger than when I started the trail. The AT had literally reshaped my feet, and the change was permanent.

We finally found the boots I wanted at a different sporting goods store, where the manager peppered me with questions about the trail. Afterward, we grabbed a late lunch at Olive Garden and then did some grocery shopping. I picked up six days' worth of food for myself and another four days for Stephanie to send ahead to my next resupply point at the Delaware Water Gap.

That evening, Stephanie watched me closely while I half-heartedly watched TV in the motel room. I could tell she was worried. I still didn't feel quite right, but I was determined to keep going and finish the AT this season. She only had one more day of vacation before she had to head back home, and soon I'd be on my own again. Even I had to admit, it was a little unsettling to feel this worn out after a week of slack-packing through a relatively easy section of the trail.

May 30, 2012 – Wednesday

Determined to make up for lost time, I was up at 5:45 a.m. and on the trail by 7:00 a.m., thanks to Stephanie's drop-off. It had rained overnight, leaving the trail wet and muddy, so I wore my old boots to spare the new ones from a rough christening. As usual for Pennsylvania, the trail alternated between rocky stretches and outright boulder scrambles, but nothing extreme, just enough to make my feet ache.

There was a steep, rocky descent into Duncannon, where the AT runs straight down High Street for a couple of miles before reaching the bridge over the Juniata and then the Susquehanna River. A peregrine falcon was nesting on a light pole there; I'd heard it sometimes dive-bombed hikers, but it left me alone.

From there, I climbed Peter's Mountain—more boulders, more endless rocks—but I was happy to realize I was making good time. Maybe I was past whatever had knocked me down the last couple of days. When I had a little over four miles left to reach PA 225, I texted Stephanie with a 3:45 p.m. ETA. The trail smoothed out, and I ended up arriving an hour early, only to find she was already there waiting.

She'd brought along gallon jugs of water and stashed them on the trail as trail magic for other hikers. With the heat, she worried someone else might be struggling like I had been.

That night we had dinner and then watched *Powder* at the motel. It was our last night together as she'd be driving back to Buffalo after dropping me off in the morning. We tried not to dwell on the separation, but it hung in the air between us.

Chapter 6

Trouble

Pennsylvania / New Jersey / New York

May 31, 2012 – Thursday

For the first time since starting my hike two and a half months earlier, I woke up with absolutely no desire to return to the AT. I loved my ten days with Stephanie and didn't want to see her go. I kept asking myself: *Should I really be walking through the woods, or should I go home and start a new chapter of my life with her?*

The doubts were relentless. What was the purpose of this hike, anyway? I knew exactly what awaited me on the trail, and I didn't want to face it. Was I still sick, or had that illness been some kind of message to get off the trail? Maybe it was even psychosomatic, a physical expression of my doubts.

We packed up in silence and went to breakfast. Stephanie tried to look confident, but I knew she was worried about my health and emotional state. I didn't want to disappoint her by admitting I didn't want to hike anymore, not after everything she had done to support me. We kept our conversation to minor pleasantries, both of us pretending to be cheerful while hiding miserable hearts.

At the trailhead on PA 225 we smiled, hugged tightly, said our fake-cheery goodbyes, and went our separate ways.

The trail was exactly as bad as I feared with rocks everywhere, which forced me to keep my head down to avoid tripping, but I missed all the scenery. My pace was slow. I wondered if I had gotten spoiled by slack-packing or if something deeper was wrong. My new boots were fine, but my same old feet still hurt. Was I really capable of hiking three more months like this? My thoughts looped in an endless litany of doubt.

I stopped for lunch at a creek along Highway 325. Normally, a spot like that would calm me, but I couldn't shake the spiral of questions in my head. I doubted I'd make it to Rausch Gap Shelter by 6 p.m., but despite everything, I arrived at 5:30 p.m. Still, it didn't lift my spirits. The shelter was under reconstruction, so I had to camp in a coal-littered clearing that looked ancient. Even with a level tent site and a surprisingly good water source (rare for Pennsylvania), I couldn't break free of my gloom.

A family group arrived later but kept to themselves, which only magnified my loneliness. Why hadn't I found a hiking partner like so many others? At least slack-packing gave me conversations with Stephanie at the end of each day. I tried texting her, but the signal was poor.

I went through the motions—ate, cleaned up, then sat on a grassy spot near the shelter. The overcast sky softened the heat, and the forest around me was lush, as if reclaiming what had once been a coal mine. Slowly, the green quieted my mind. So what if I was alone? I had just shared a wonderful week with Stephanie, I had talked with my family, and now I was here in this peaceful place.

By nightfall, I surprised myself by feeling content. For the first time on the AT, I fully relaxed in my sleeping bag and drifted into a deep, restful sleep. My "Day of Doubt" was over.

June 1, 2012 – Friday

I woke at 5:15 a.m. to a beautiful morning and was back on the trail by 6:30 a.m. One advantage of being alone was I didn't have to wait on anyone. Stephanie had texted me a warning about severe thunderstorms with hail, so I pushed to reach the 501 Shelter by early afternoon.

The morning climb was steady but gentle. After crossing I-80 and a few roads, I began ascending yet another Blue Mountain (seemed every state had one). For once, the rocks were scattered, and even some stretches were flat. I made good time and arrived at the 501 Shelter by 2:30 p.m., just as the rain began.

The 501 was a round cabin with a skylight, table, and six double bunks, which was a luxury by Pennsylvania standards. Shelters here were few and far between, often down side trails, but this one was the exception and right off the trail so I stayed, especially with the storm rolling in.

It was already crowded with hikers, but I managed to snag a top bunk. Chatting with others, I learned that Plus-Two was back on the trail and a day ahead. I texted him, though it was a disappointment to be behind.

As the rain poured, more hikers crammed in. By nightfall, there were twenty people in a cabin built for twelve.

Still, the mood was light. A German hiker named Achy Breaky showed up. I hadn't seen him since Georgia, and we swapped stories. Someone ordered pizza delivery, and boxes kept arriving. Despite the storm and cramped quarters, we spent the evening playing cards, talking, and laughing. I was grateful to be indoors; it would have been a miserable night in a tent.

June 2, 2012 – Saturday

I set out at 6:30 a.m., before most hikers stirred. The rocks returned quickly, joined by a new hazard—water. With all the rain, the trail itself had become a stream. At first, it was just damp, then ankle-deep, then completely flowing. In some stretches, I had no choice but to run through it, and once I even lost the poorly marked trail.

The wet conditions aggravated the healing blister on my toe until the pain was unbearable. By lunch near Route 183, I hurt so badly I wanted to cry. I wrote in my journal: *The AT is miserable, and so am I.*

I tried drying my feet, treating the blister, and taking anti-inflammatories, but nothing helped. Hobbling onward, I eventually reached Eagle's Nest Shelter and set up my tent. A few familiar hikers were there, including Trail Mix, Parson John (a minister I'd just met the night before at 501), and Willy Boy, whom I hadn't seen since Maryland. Their company lifted my spirits for a while, though my infected toe dominated my thoughts. I did my best to clean out the abscess, but a day in soaked boots had only made things worse.

That night I called Stephanie. I told her about my flooded boots, the swollen blister, the painful straps on my new pack, the cramps in my right leg, and the bone bruise on one foot from Pennsylvania's endless sharp rocks. Of the fifteen miles I'd hiked that day, only two had been free of obstacles. She urged me to see a doctor in Port Clinton.

I admitted I was drowning in doubt, even fantasizing about walking off the trail and catching a bus home. Realizing how bleak I sounded, I tried to lighten the mood. I told her how much I enjoyed talking with the hikers that night, and I finished with a joke: at least my pack was getting lighter every day as I ate through my food!

June 3, 2012 – Sunday

I had planned a long 23.8-mile day. The first 8 miles weren't too bad; my work draining the toe abscess seemed to have helped, though I still needed anti-inflammatories to manage the pain. Of course, Pennsylvania's rocks were ever-present, but it was manageable until I hit the descent into Port Clinton. The AT dropped almost straight down, rock to rock, and when I finally reached the bottom, I found myself walking through what felt like a deserted town. For two miles, I passed parked cars but saw no people. Was everyone in church? Had something happened? I kept walking, puzzled, until I later learned the whole town had gone to an event on the Schuylkill River.

After crossing Route 61, I climbed yet another Blue Mountain and reached Windsor Furnace Shelter. It was tempting to stay, but it was only 2:00 p.m., so I pushed on. I almost regretted it because the next three miles around Pulpit Overlook were covered in rocks and poorly blazed. I didn't bother with the overlook, though I heard the view of Hawk Mountain was beautiful. Soon, the trail opened onto a wide forest road crowded with day hikers.

I raced the rain to Eckville Shelter and lost, arriving soaked. Because it was a watershed area, camping wasn't allowed, so we all crammed into the converted garage—six bunks, a shower, and hikers everywhere. I was glad to see Hawkeye again and caught up with The Dude, Trail Mix, G. Pa, and Buzzkill with his dog, Greta. Four new faces rounded out the group.

Being close to Auburn, we had the luxury of ordering delivery. I splurged on a Philly cheesesteak. It took over an hour to arrive, and I was starving, but when it finally came, the whole shelter turned into a little party. Beds were full, so I dragged a bench against a wall ledge, stretched out on it, and made do. My feet ached all night, and Buzzkill's dog kept waking me up, but at least it had been a fun evening.

June 4, 2012 – Monday

I set out at 7:00 a.m. on wet rocks courtesy of last night's storm. Pennsylvania didn't disappoint—besides four boulder fields, the trail was covered in what I called "nuisance rocks." The worst part was Knife Edge, a razor-thin stretch with drop-offs on both sides. I ended up sitting and sliding across sections, unsure of my balance.

By some miracle, I reached Bake Oven Knob Shelter just in time to set up before the rain started. My feet were wrecked, my hips ached, and my back screamed from all the slips and saves I'd made thanks to my trekking poles. I was angry at Pennsylvania, angry at the maintainers, angry at the endless sharp rocks. Still, I grimaced and told myself I would beat this trail. I had to make the pain mean something.

June 5, 2012 – Tuesday

Originally, I'd planned to resupply in Palmerton, but between Stephanie's send-off breakfast and the cheesesteak delivery, I had an extra day of food. I decided to push hard and try to reach Delaware Water Gap, where Stephanie had mailed a resupply package, before running out. That meant a couple of 20+ mile days, and my body complained in advance, but I committed.

I aimed for Leroy A. Smith Shelter, 23.4 miles away. The first seven miles were really hard with five boulder fields, including the Lehigh Gap Climb, which required hand-over-hand scrambling with a full pack. The view was amazing but nerve-wracking, the valley stretching below with towns, roads, and an old steel plant; nature reclaiming human industry.

A three-mile grassy road gave me a breather before the rocks returned. Along the way I passed the body of a fawn, a sad counterpoint to the endless stone. I figured 80% of the trail that day was rocks. This was my first true rock climb on the AT, but I knew it wouldn't be my last.

At lunch, Trail Mix caught up, then disappeared again, only to reappear later setting up camp. I pressed on, finally reaching the shelter by 6:00 p.m., rewarded with trail magic sodas, two of which I gratefully downed. Hawkeye, Q, and Keeps Going were already there, and later Spice Rack (Brooke) showed up. I hadn't seen him since Georgia, and we caught up, with me bragging about Stephanie's support.

Others mentioned a strangely tame fawn they'd passed earlier. When I told them about the carcass I'd seen, we realized the odd behavior must have been illness. It was dark, wet, and rough in the shelter, but the company lifted my spirits.

June 6, 2012 – Wednesday

I hit the trail at 6:30 a.m., and it was rocks for eight solid hours. I kept my head down, watching every step, until I finally reached the Delaware Water Gap.

I almost missed the turn, but some locals redirected me before I wandered too far. I made it to town in time to grab my resupply package and checked into the church hostel, grateful for a shower.

Clean at last, I called Stephanie. She heard the discouragement in my voice as I listed my aches: a new, searing pain along the outside of my right leg from knee to hip. She suspected it was my ilio-tibial (IT) band, aggravated by my old knee issues. I could hear the worry in her voice, though she tried not to discourage me. I, too, wondered if I was damaging myself beyond repair.

That night I sat with the other hostel hikers, including Tortoise Chef, Beast, Spider, Standing Indian, and Molasses. We shared leftover pizza and trail food. The hostel was bare bones: wooden pallets for beds, our pads and bags the only comfort. The company was good, but I couldn't shake the gloom. Vitamin I didn't touch the ache in my hip, knee, and IT band. My sleep was broken by pain, by Tortoise Chef's thunderous snoring, and by the same doubts that haunted me every night.

June 7, 2012 – Thursday

The poor night's sleep kept me in bed later than usual, but eventually I packed up and walked to the Water Gap Diner. Tarzan was there with his girlfriend, and we shared breakfast. The food and conversation lifted my spirits, and I returned to the hostel to shoulder my pack in a better mood.

The trail wound through town, crossed the Delaware River, and followed park roads for an easy start. At the Delaware Water Gap National Recreation Center on Kittatinny Mountain, I stopped to chat with a park ranger who was curious about hiking the AT. She was kind, attentive, and, if I'm honest, very cute. I even noted in my journal that she was "one of the Park's finest."

Once the trail left the road for the woods, the rocks returned, and I slowed down. Tarzan had warned me it would be rocky for another two and a half miles. The ridge offered views of the Delaware River on one side and lakes and reservoirs on the other. Crossing the river meant leaving Pennsylvania behind and adding New Jersey to my list of states hiked, but I only managed 10.5 miles that day. My body protested after the poor night of sleep, and I simply didn't feel well.

I stopped at the AMC Mohican Outdoor Center. The campsite was damp and disappointing, but there was clean water, which was hard to come by in that polluted area.

I was grateful for my AMC membership discount, though I had expected better. At least the lake view gave me something to appreciate. As soon as I stopped hiking the leg pain returned. I switched to aspirin, since ibuprofen had failed me the night before, and went to bed early, hoping rest would help.

June 8, 2012 - Friday

Despite turning in early, I hardly slept and gave up at 5 a.m. I was exhausted but determined, annoyed at myself for covering only ten miles the previous day. I set a target of Gren Anderson Shelter, a full twenty miles ahead. The rocks still dominated the trail, but there were merciful stretches of smoother ground and a few easy miles along old roads. Leaving at dawn gave me the gift of seeing several deer. I also considered that although my legs were tired, the sharp pain had eased.

Trail magic lifted my spirits when I met a weekend hiker named Snores at a parking area. He handed me apples and a drink and told me that he and his friend Don would be near Gren Anderson that night. He confessed his trail name was well-earned, and out of courtesy, he always camped away from other hikers.

The day's ridge walk brought views of lakes and rivers. The steel bridge at Culvers Gap stood out, but I was too drained to enjoy it. I reached my destination on schedule but felt "off." It was unsettling to me how quickly my strength seemed to fade. Was it all in my head? Was I weak, or was something truly wrong with me?

At least I had a cell signal to call Stephanie and wish her a happy birthday. She was thrilled about the flowers I had arranged through my son-in-law, Gregg. Knowing I made her smile brightened my day. Later, I set up camp, ate, and spent some time talking with Snores and Don. Snores even shared a bit of bourbon.

Around 8:30 p.m. I heard someone call "Yo Hoot!" At first, I thought Snores was joking, but it turned out to be Plus-Two. He had taken a break off the trail and gotten behind me again. I had texted him earlier with my plans, and he had pushed a thirty-mile day just to catch up with me. Hearing his voice and seeing his smile felt like a blessing. I knew then I wouldn't be walking alone.

June 9, 2012 - Saturday

We set out together at 6:45 the next morning, planning an eighteen-mile hike to the Jim Murray Property, a small cabin near Gemmer Road that word-of-mouth claimed was open to thru-hikers. The morning started rocky but eased after High Point Shelter. At High Point—the highest elevation in New Jersey—we stopped at the visitor center, climbed the tower, and took pictures. When I removed my hat, I discovered a tick on my forehead. Over the course of the day, I pulled off six more. Hiking through brush made me uneasy; the ticks were relentless, and I much preferred the shaded woods.

Hiking with Plus-Two lifted my spirits. I had never minded solitude, but companionship made the miles pass faster. Still, I couldn't ignore how hard it was to keep up with him. He had always walked at a quicker pace, but this time the effort stressed me more than usual.

We nearly missed the Jim Murray cabin because it wasn't marked. Inside, we found Ron from Canada and a thru-hiker named Dark Ages. The place was compact but efficient, with every corner put to use. The shower was nothing more than a spigot over stones outside, but it felt wonderful. After eating, I collapsed into sleep, completely spent.

June 10, 2012 - Sunday

Another terrible night followed. Pain ran through my legs and back, and ibuprofen did nothing. I added aspirin, which dulled it enough for some rest, but I woke heavy and tired. We left at 6 a.m.. Being first on the trail meant clearing spider webs, and Plus-Two and I took turns at "point."

We walked into Unionville, New York, where we grabbed breakfast sandwiches, donuts, and coffee. I was absurdly grateful for that simple cup of coffee. I also used the general store to resupply for two more days. Back on the trail, we moved well through a mix of rocky stretches and steady rain. Along the way, I saw my first bear, a young one wandering down the path. I shouted "Bear!" to Plus-Two, but it darted off before I could take a picture.

The climb up Pochuck Mountain led us to a long boardwalk through the swamp. Locals used the area for jogging, and two women passed us, leaving behind the faint scent of soap or perfume. I inhaled dramatically and told Plus-Two, "Ah, the scent of a woman!" He laughed the first time, but shut me down when I repeated it after the joggers passed again. We still chuckled about it as their fragrance lingered in the air behind them.

At Glenwood, New Jersey, we stopped at a roadside garden center that, to our delight, sold food, drinks, and ice cream. I ordered Maine Blueberry, which gave me a little boost before the punishing climb up Wawayanda Mountain.

We reached Wawayanda Shelter by 5 p.m. Soon, other hikers gathered: Master Splinter, Laces, and Sid, a young section hiker. Master Splinter had befriended some local kids who showed up with food, drinks, and two huge dogs. They peppered us with questions about the trail before heading home before dark. That night, when I complained of my aching back, Master Splinter offered me a muscle relaxer. I accepted gratefully and slept better than I had in days, even as the rain pattered down outside.

June 11, 2012 – Monday

Hiking with another early bird made it easy for me to be up and out by 6:30 a.m. I loved the early mornings. We planned on using the restroom at the park headquarters, but it was locked, so we both headed for the woods. I rarely needed to use the woods, since I carefully stopped where there were privies, but this was one of those times where it was necessary.

Plus-Two worried about his timing to finish the thru-hike because of family commitments, so he decided to do a 27-mile day. I knew I just couldn't physically keep that pace, and we would have to part ways. With the pressure off, I decided to try a shorter day to rest my legs and back and hopefully ease the constant pain.

The twelve-mile walk was miserable. The rocks returned as the trail left New Jersey and entered my home state of New York; state #9 on the trail. I had hoped the trail would somehow be better here, but it was just as bad as everywhere else. I fell three times that day, each fall jarring my knees, one leaving a bloody brush burn. Up until then, I'd only fallen twice (the knee twist and the "turtle" with Plus-Two in Virginia), so three falls in one day meant something was wrong. At least it was sunny, though my gear was still wet and needed airing.

At one point, I climbed over a rock and heard a loud hissing noise. *A huge rattlesnake.* Suddenly, it dawned on me that the buzzing sound I'd been hearing all along wasn't cicadas, but rattlesnake tails. Eastern rattlers don't rattle like the western ones I knew from TV; they buzz. Backing away, my heart pounded thinking of how many I must have passed without realizing.

I made it to Wildcat Shelter, cleaned up my knee, and called Stephanie. As I told her about the little bear from the day before, I froze. "And... there is another one. A big one. There's a bear coming right at me …" She held her breath until I said, "and now it's moving away." This one was much larger and had little concern about me. Thankfully, my food was already stored in the bear box.

Stephanie listened carefully. She'd been worried since Delaware Water Gap, and hearing about my falls solidified her conviction that something was wrong. I told her how excited I was to see my son Nathan the next day. He lived in Highland Falls near West Point and had offered to help me slack-pack while the AT was within his driving range. Stephanie secretly decided to surprise me by coming too, arranging it with Nathan after we hung up.

Unaware of her plan, I set out my bag, spread out my damp gear, and tried not to dwell on the disappointment of losing Plus-Two's company. Pragmatically, I knew I couldn't keep up. Stephanie's concerns echoed in my head, and I decided to go slow the next day, just enough to get within Nathan's reach, then take a Zero. Another hiker showed up before dark, and I felt relieved. Knowing there was a big bear around was less frightening with company.

June 12, 2012 – Tuesday

Pain woke me around 5 a.m., so I hit the trail early, planning to walk until I could call Nathan. The climbs were hand-over-hand rock scrambles. I hated them. My pace was under two miles an hour, frustratingly slow.

I stopped at Harriman State Park for lunch just as the rain began. Wet rocks meant extra caution. I reached Arden Valley Rd., the first pickup point, but it was too early for Nathan, so I pushed two more miles to Seven Lakes Drive. By then, I'd done over 17 miles, sick, wet, and sore, though the terrain had been fairly easy. Something just wasn't right.

When Nate called to say he couldn't be there until 6 p.m., I waited by the road, shivering, then walked to stay warm until he found me near a lake. It was wonderful to see him again. He laughed at my "hiker stink," hurried me into the shower, and threw my filthy clothes into the laundry while I wore his big bathrobe. He was shocked by my weight loss. Then came chicken wings, pizza, and ice cream! I ate and ate until I finally felt full.

I called Stephanie, and she told me she'd see me that weekend at Nathan's. Relaxed, I went to bed but woke shortly after midnight with severe back pain. A muscle relaxer, aspirin, and finally ibuprofen got me through until morning. Thankfully, I had already planned a Zero.

June 13, 2012 – Wednesday (Zero)

The Zero was blissful. I was clean, comfortable, and with my son. We talked, watched Euro Cup Soccer, and capped the night with a movie, *John Carter*. I planned to hike again the next day, but another night of this unusual back pain kept me up until 4:30 a.m.

June 14, 2012 – Thursday

The painful night pushed me toward another Zero, but oddly, after my morning coffee, the pain eased. I decided to hike. Nathan drove me back to the AT around 10 a.m., and I decided to slack-pack this time.

The hike began easily, with some hand-over-hand climbs. Bear Mountain, surprisingly, wasn't bad at all, and most of it was stairs and gravel, more tourist path than trail. I had been there the year before when Stephanie and I helped Nathan move, so it felt familiar. I took photos from the top.

The AT passed through a small zoo before crossing the Bear Mountain Bridge, which was a long, beautiful span, then it climbed steeply on the far side. By the time I reached South Mountain Pass Rd., I'd done 14.5 miles and called for pickup. Back at the apartment, I showered, ate, and cleaned the kitchen to do my part.

June 15, 2012 – Friday

Despite another poor night's sleep, I stuck with the plan. Nathan dropped me at South Mountain Pass Rd. The blazes were sparse, forcing me to stop often to scout the trail.

At a deli gas station near Rte. 403 & 9, I ran into Trail Mix and Hawkeye. Trail Mix and I compared our New York injuries, both griping about the trail. After lunch, the hiking was surprisingly easy, making us liars about how bad NY was.

I passed Graymoor Friary but pressed on, later regretting not stopping. Hawkeye and I leapfrogged along the trail. Eventually, I reached Fahnestock State Park around 4:30 p.m. and called for pickup. Hawkeye caught a ride with us to a campsite.

Slack-packing made the miles easier, and a belly full of pizza should have brought sleep, but instead my back tightened again, forcing me to pace through the night.

June 16, 2012 – Saturday (Zero)

With no sleep and constant pain, I took another Zero. Stephanie arrived at 4:00 p.m., and I was overjoyed to see her! She hadn't seen me since Pennsylvania and was startled by how bad I looked. She tried massage and comfort, but her instincts said something was seriously wrong. When pain woke me again that night, she insisted I see a doctor.

June 17, 2012 – Sunday (Zero)

By 6 a.m. I was in enough pain to agree. Stephanie drove me to St. Luke's Hospital in Cornwall, the only place open. They ran blood and urine tests, a CT scan, and, thanks to her pushing, also tested for Lyme disease. She'd read in her vet journals about a spike in cases along the northeast corridor and knew I'd had tick encounters.

The nurse, Michael, was wonderful. After four hours, the diagnosis came back: dehydration and constipation, with evidence of a deteriorating disc. I was shocked. I'd been drinking and moving my bowels regularly, but apparently not enough.

I left with painkillers and stool softeners. Back at Nathan's, I slept the afternoon away. When I woke, Stephanie brought food, and the three of us watched *Sherlock Holmes 2*. That night, finally, I slept well.

June 18, 2012 – Monday (Zero)

I decided to continue my recovery with another Zero, hoping it would get me back to normal. Nate had the day off, so we hung out together, chatting and watching TV. Stephanie drove me to Walmart for supplies and took me out for lunch, but otherwise we stayed in the apartment all day. I still didn't feel 100%, but I resolved to hike the next day anyway, hoping the improvement would continue.

June 19, 2012 – Tuesday

Stephanie dropped me off at the AT by 8:00 a.m. I hiked around Canopus Lake feeling pretty good, though a little tired. I figured it was because I had taken so many Zeros and lost my trail legs. The trail was rocky but manageable, so I was surprised when I calculated my mileage and saw how poor my pace was.

I stopped at RPH Shelter for lunch and was delighted when Mouse showed up. I hadn't seen her since Shenandoah. We caught up, and I told her about my hospital trip. She and two other hikers were heading to a deli off Rt. 52 and invited me along, but I had to decline, as I was way behind schedule. I'd planned for Stephanie to pick me up at Rt. 55, but I called to change it to Rt. 52 instead.

By the time I reached it, I was completely exhausted after just 12.5 miles. Back at Nate's, I showered and ate dinner before settling in for the night. Then the hospital called to tell me the blood test for Lyme disease was positive! At last, my crushing exhaustion had an explanation. Honestly, the real wonder was that I'd been able to hike at all.

Stephanie found a late-night pharmacy and filled my doxycycline prescription so I could start immediately. She was worried about how long I'd had the disease, since the longer it went untreated, the more likely long-term complications would follow. Thinking back to the "heat stroke" in Pennsylvania and the tick she'd pulled off me in Virginia, it was possible I'd been infected for six weeks or more. The doctor prescribed the longer course of antibiotics; four weeks total.

Unfortunately, doxycycline causes sun-sensitivity, and hiking in the sun was now out of the question. Even if I'd wanted to keep going, I couldn't risk it. The trail would have to wait four weeks.

June 20, 2012 – Wednesday (Driving home)

Stephanie and I left early, before Nathan woke up, for the 5½-hour drive back to Buffalo. I sat in silence; lost in thoughts I couldn't escape. Taking a month off meant I wouldn't finish a thru-hike this year. Would I ever recover? Would I be one of those people debilitated by Lyme forever?

I knew if Stephanie hadn't intervened, I would've kept forcing myself forward. I was grateful she got me to the hospital and insisted I stop, though part of me resented not having a choice. What if I couldn't return to the AT? What if I didn't want to? The self-doubt churned in my head the whole ride, making me feel like a failure.

When we arrived, I surprised Sarah and Larissa with my return, then explained the Lyme diagnosis. Since Sarah was living in my house, I stayed with Stephanie.

I didn't believe in living together without marriage, but I was too sick and discouraged to argue.

That night, I ended my daily hiking journal with: *"Any further entries will be when I resume hiking."* I had finished about 1,400 miles, which was almost two-thirds of the trail. I forced myself to think of it as "when," not "if." Anything else was too depressing.

Chapter 7

Tenacity Together

New York / Connecticut / Massachusetts

Interlude – June-July 2012

Much of the next month was a blur for me. I was sicker and more debilitated than I'd realized. Lyme disease had been quietly destroying my system, and I'd pushed my body too far. Exhaustion consumed me. While Stephanie went to work each day, I slept.

One day during that first week, she came home, and I told her I had staggered downstairs for a glass of water but was too weak to climb back up without nearly falling. I'd had to creep up the stairs. This from the same man who had once hiked 28 miles in a day with my Shenandoah crew, or crossed mountains on what I used to call "short days."

Stephanie drove us to her parents' place on Cape Cod for a week's vacation, but I barely remember it. I was too tired to help drive or enjoy the trip—just sleeping or sitting in a chair, dulled by fatigue. At home, she kept me fed and offered quiet company when she wasn't working. Slowly, I began to improve. I could stay awake for parts of the day and even make it downstairs to the recliner to watch TV. Her cats seemed to enjoy having me around.

Still, I worried about the random pains like the burning in my feet, the strange numbness despite barely walking at all. Stephanie took me to an infectious disease doctor who questioned the Lyme diagnosis. My labs showed I was positive for seven of ten Lyme subsets. To her, that was "close enough," and since the doxycycline seemed to be working, we stayed the course.

Recovery took the full four weeks. I hadn't even realized the mental fog I'd been in until one day I told Stephanie, "I can think again." She knew I was better when she came home to find I'd painted a wall in her bathroom. I told her I "had to earn my keep," and before long, I was tackling projects around her house, painting the dining room, power-washing the patio, cleaning the garage and the basement. I seemed to forget I was supposed to be resting.

As my last week on antibiotics began, I started making plans to return to the trail. If I wanted any hope of reaching Mt. Katahdin before Baxter State Park closed, I had to move fast. Stephanie had her doubts, but we compromised—she'd take time off work to slack-pack me at first, carrying my big pack in her car so I could ease back in. Nathan offered his house in Highland Falls, New York, as my starting point, so the weekend after finishing antibiotics, we drove there.

July 22, 2012 – Sunday (Driving back to the AT)

That morning, we went to my church before leaving. I was touched by how many people wished me luck and promised to keep me in their prayers. It lifted me to know they cared about my dream.

I felt well enough to drive the whole way to Nathan's. Stephanie read aloud or we chatted. We stopped for dinner at the Park Restaurant in Highland Falls, then let ourselves into Nate's place as planned. He was away that weekend, which meant I could turn in early.

July 23, 2012 – Monday

Stephanie isn't a morning person, so the 5:30 a.m. wake-up was rough for her, but I was up and ready, daypack in hand. She watched me slip back into "Hoot" mode. After breakfast at Andy's Restaurant, she drove me to the spot on Route 52 where I'd left the AT last month. Rain started as we pulled up, worsening the moment she stopped—classic Hoot weather.

I stepped back onto the trail at 9:00 a.m. It felt surreal after almost five weeks away. Luckily, this section was easy, with gentle climbs and clear white blazes. By late morning, I met another hiker, Stumbles, who had started the AT on May 7, exactly two months after me. It hit me how much ground I'd lost. My March-start peers were now far ahead, some even finished.

After nine rainy miles, the sun came out at Nuclear Lake, and I stopped for lunch. I called Stephanie to say I should reach Route 22 by about 4:00 p.m., but the trail stayed smooth, so I arrived early. She pulled up at the exact same time, having guessed I would walk faster than I'd expected. I called her the "master of good timing."

We drove back to Nate's, giving Stumbles a ride. I was thrilled I'd covered nearly 15 miles at a good pace without major problems. After cleaning up, we went out for Mexican food, then watched *The Big Year* before turning in at 10 p.m., late by hiker standards, but I wasn't worried. Tomorrow, I'd be back at it again.

July 24, 2012 – Tuesday

Stephanie and I were up and out by 6 a.m., stopping for breakfast at Karen's, a little restaurant near the AT. I started hiking around 8:20 a.m. The walk had more ups and downs than yesterday, but the path was clear, and the rain held off. Along the way, I met a hiker named Croc Hunter who thought he might have a tick bite. I told him about my own experience and urged him to get it checked. It felt good to think my bad luck might help someone else avoid the same fate.

By 11 a.m., I crossed into my 10th state, Connecticut, finally leaving New York behind. I love my home state, but being sick for most of that stretch colored my experience. I stopped at Ten Mile Creek for lunch around 12:30 p.m. and called Stephanie. She was already at Bulls Bridge Road waiting for me, having a good sense now of my pace. She'd been admiring the covered bridge nearby. I reached her around 1:15 p.m., wrapping up a short 11.3-mile day. We'd agreed to keep things easy, so I didn't burn out after just recovering.

We took the scenic route back to Nathan's, had pizza for dinner, then walked to the Thayer Hotel to see Nate working at the Zulu Time Bar and thank him for letting us use his apartment. After a drink, we headed back for an early night.

July 25, 2012 – Wednesday

That morning, we packed up. I was too far up the trail now to keep using Nate's place, and we didn't want to overstay our welcome. After one last breakfast at Andy's, Stephanie drove me to Connecticut. I was back on the trail by 8:20 a.m.

It was a peaceful day, no wind as I ascended Schaghticoke Mountain. The AT wound along the NY/CT border past the Schaghticoke Indian Reservation. A short climb to Indian Rocks gave me a sweeping view. I had lunch at Mt. Algo Shelter and texted Stephanie, who turned out to be nearby at Route 341. I walked on to meet her for a quick break, grateful to see her mid-day.

Afterward, I climbed Skiff Mountain and Caleb's Peak, taking plenty of photos of the view that still couldn't match the real thing. The descent at St. John's Ledges was really hard, almost straight down on rock steps. (Later, I'd laugh that I thought this so difficult, but I didn't know then that worse was ahead.) At the bottom, the trail followed the Housatonic River for five wonderfully flat miles.

Halfway through, Stephanie appeared! She'd parked at the rendezvous and hiked two miles back to meet me, teasing that with three AT miles under her belt now, she might be a section hiker. She'd even run into Stumbles in town and given him rides for supplies. We walked together to the end of the River Road section, chatting easily.

Stephanie had booked a motel close to the trail. Even slack-packing, 16.5 miles with two mountain climbs, left me wiped out. After a quick nap, we went out for Chinese food.

July 26, 2012 – Thursday

With bad weather coming, we planned a short day. Breakfast was leftover Chinese before Stephanie dropped me at the trailhead. The route was a series of steep climbs and sharp descents, hard on my feet and knees. The strange pain in the bottoms of my feet I'd felt while so sick was back, on top of my chronic knee pain. My resolve wavered; I couldn't muster the passion I'd had starting out.

The weather gave me an excuse to stop at Sharon Mountain Road after just 8.5 miles. The road was barely passable, but Stephanie managed to drive her car through the woods to collect me and get us back to the motel, where I fell asleep instantly. She later took me to a nice dinner at the Black Goose, trying to lift my dark mood. My dream of a thru-hike felt like it was slipping away, but I wasn't ready to quit.

July 27, 2012 – Friday

Stephanie braved that awful road again to drop me at the trail by 7:20 a.m. The rest had helped, and the terrain was gentler—gradual uphills, quick downhills.

I made great time to Route 7, my mood lifting with each mile. I passed through Falls Village, climbed Prospect Mountain for another good view, and tried to be fully present, focusing on the beauty even under gray skies. I reached Route 41 in Salisbury, where Stephanie was waiting, then pushed on another mile to stick to my plan. It had been a good day.

Back at the motel, I did laundry, forgetting my flip-phone was in my shorts pocket. It didn't survive the wash. The hotel clerk gave us dried daal (as the closest thing to rice) to pack it in, hoping it would dry out. Then my daughter called: my home water bill was $600, thanks to a leaking toilet. My good mood tanked.

Stephanie rescued the evening with a "date night" at the same fancy restaurant, both of us dressed up. Despite the day's setbacks, I relaxed and remembered just how lucky I was to have her with me on this journey.

July 28, 2012 – Saturday

Stephanie was on my hiker schedule, so we were up early. With few food options, we ate at the surprisingly good General Store, where I also grabbed a sandwich for lunch. She dropped me at the trail by 7 a.m., and the day started strong.

The morning climb up Riga and Bear Mountains went smoothly. I prefer knocking out mountains early, while I still have energy. I finished the Connecticut section along Sage Ravine and stepped into my 11th state, Massachusetts. That's when things turned ugly. The AT here was rocky, and as I climbed Race Mountain, rain began. The trail ran along a steep ridge with a valley drop-off. By the time I left the mountain, thunder rolled in, and rain poured harder.

The ascent up Mt. Everett was a rock path turned into a stream. Past the summit, the trail was steep and slippery. I ducked into Glen Brook Shelter for lunch and chatted with a southbound hiker about my Lyme disease.

Meanwhile, Stephanie was watching the weather with growing concern. With my phone dead, we had no way to communicate. She waited at our first pick-up spot, passing the time with the *Thru-Hiker's Handbook*, and discovered the section I was in was considered dangerous when wet. One hiker had even been helicoptered out, she read. When two hikers approached, she asked if they'd seen "Hoot." One said yes … in Virginia. It turned out they were the two hikers named Coach I'd told her about months earlier. She wished them well and retreated to the dry car to wait.

I left Glen Brook feeling good, but the downhill from Jug End was a nightmare with wet rock faces in heavy rain, fading blazes, and one slip that forced me to grab trees to stop a fall. By the time I reached Route 41 in South Egremont, I was soaked but in one piece. Stephanie jumped out to hug me, relief written all over her face.

It had been a 17.8-mile day. We drove to Lee, MA, where she'd found a motel. My phone had mostly dried out, though the mic was dead, so we stopped at Verizon for an earpiece. I still refused to upgrade from my flip phone. When I finished the AT, maybe then I'd splurge on a smartphone. We had dinner at Old Country Buffet, then wound down watching *Independence Day* at the motel.

July 29, 2012 – Sunday

Stephanie returned me to Route 41 after a quick motel breakfast. The first 4.5 miles were flat and easy, though steady rain made the rocks slick on East Mountain. I reached Tom Leonard Shelter by 12:30 p.m. for lunch.

I'd skipped anti-inflammatories to gauge the true condition of my feet. The pain was constant and draining; every step hurt. Thankfully, it was a short day: just three more miles to Blue Hill Road, though they were brutal.

Stephanie was waiting, but on the drive back, she detoured to check on a steer she'd seen loose along the road. We couldn't find it and hoped it had returned to its pasture. Back at the motel, I told her the pain was bad enough that I might have to quit. Even clean, dry socks didn't help; the bottoms of my feet were agonizing from toe pad to heel. I'd never felt anything like it, and we suspected this was related to the Lyme disease. That night, we went to the Bombay Restaurant to lift my spirits. I decided to try one more hike before making the final call.

July 30, 2012 – Monday

Another early start, another motel breakfast, then back on the trail for a short, ten-mile hike to Tyringham Road. The sun was out, the scenery was beautiful, and the trail was gentle. I rested often, trying to baby my feet. Still, the pain returned after a few miles and never let up. I knew I couldn't continue this season. My thru-hiker dream had been crushed by a stupid tick bite.

I chatted with two northbound, or NOBO hikers at Shaker Campsite about my Lyme disease and decision to stop. They congratulated me on how far I'd come, but their kind words couldn't soften the disappointment.

At Tyringham Road, I told Stephanie, "Take me home before I change my mind." She took one look at me, turned west onto the Mass Pike, and drove straight to Buffalo.

The ride home was a haze of disappointment. I felt like a failure, not just for quitting, but for slack-packing much of the way. I'd missed the camaraderie of shelters and rarely saw hikers during the day, making me feel alone. The Lyme disease, the pain, the isolation, it had all taken the joy from the trail. Still, I promised myself I'd finish the AT someday, even if I had to crawl up Katahdin.

Once home, Stephanie sent an email update to my followers. She hoped it would help me see what I had accomplished.

She wrote: *On this epic hike, he has seen bears, deer, foxes, squirrels, chipmunks, mice, rattlesnakes, a water moccasin, several rat snakes and a large variety of birds in their native habitat. He has hiked the southern Appalachian Mountains, Roan Highlands, Great Smoky Mountains, Blue Ridge Mountains, Kittatinny Range, Hudson Highlands, and the southern Berkshires. He has crossed several of the major rivers of the East Coast, including the Potomac, Shenandoah, Susquehanna, Delaware, Hudson and Housatonic to name the most famous. He has walked through 11 states; GA, TN, NC, VA, WV, MD, PA, NJ, NY, CT, and about ⅓ of MA (VT, NH and ME are left). He has met people from all walks of life, and from many states and foreign countries. He has hiked through snow, rain, and blazing heat.*

I am moved by the courage demonstrated by any individual who takes on a project of this magnitude. About 2,000 people attempt to thru-hike each year, knowing that less than 20% will be able to complete the grueling, months-long trek in one season. Each of the AT hikers has his or her own unique story, with triumphs and failures of their own. I am proud to have been able to personally support Greg/Hoot as he took on this journey, and to be able to share his story with you and report back to him all the supportive emails from so many of you.

We don't know what is next for Greg. He has a new grandson coming this month, and life has a way of making its own demands on time and attention. The Appalachian Trail may call him back once his body recovers, but this may have been the one magical time in his life when he could actually heed that call.

I wish to thank Greg for sharing the adventure of Hoot with me and with all of us. Hoot had an almost impossible dream, and acted on it to the fullest extent of his abilities. I believe a lot of us have dreams that we put aside, afraid of failing, or afraid of leaving our comfortable existence in favor of the unknown. It is inspiring to have been able to follow his daring undertaking. I am proud of you, Greg.

Thank you to every single one of you. You may not realize it, but your support had a huge impact on Greg. Your words (email, cards) gave him inspiration at the hardest parts of the trail, and kept him going on. May you all find support for the dreams in your hearts, as well

Chapter 8

Hundred Mile Honeymoon

Massachusetts / Vermont

Interlude – 2012–2013

My return to Buffalo was heralded by the birth of my third grandson, when my daughter, Larissa, welcomed her second son, Owen.

Soon after, I learned that my other daughter, Sarah, was also pregnant with her second son, expected in early 2013. Since Sarah was still living in my house, I continued staying with Stephanie.

In September, I proposed to Stephanie, with the strong support of my children. (I even let Plus-Two know I'd followed his advice. He'd listened to me rave about Stephanie along the trail and kept telling me to just marry her already!) My son Jarrod recommended a local jeweler, and together Stephanie and I designed rings with our initials woven in a Celtic-style pattern of white and yellow gold. I brought in old jewelry to sell, and I made sure my father's wedding band was melted down into mine. On November 21st, I walked Stephanie to the end of a long pier on the Niagara River, just under the Peace Bridge, and asked for her hand with a ring made by that same jeweler.

Over the winter, I tried to stay in shape, but even casual walks caused foot pain. Stephanie had researched Lyme disease and discovered that peripheral neuropathy sometimes developed, which fit my symptoms. A doctor also diagnosed a bone bruise. I kept hoping everything would heal before summer 2013 so I could finish the trail.

That spring, when I received the ATC *Journeys* magazine listing all the new "2,000 milers," I felt both pride and longing. There were tears in my eyes and a smile on my lips as I read the names of Steve-O, Blue, Mouse, Rainbow, and Plus-Two. My dear friends had all completed their thru-hikes. By now, we were Facebook friends, and I copied their summit photos and pinned them to my refrigerator as inspiration. I continued to train, and slowly the foot pain improved.

Stephanie and I were married in early June at a local Episcopalian church. (My Catholic priest wouldn't allow the ceremony in his church because Stephanie wasn't Catholic, but he did join the Episcopalian service, so we ended up doubly married.) All of our children played a role in our wedding. Nathan was my best man, Jarrod played music, and Larissa, Sarah, and Stephanie's son, Bryan, gave readings. Bryan and Jarrod's wives, both seven months pregnant, were glowing reminders of more grandchildren to come. Blue and his wife Debbie, whom Stephanie had met in Harpers Ferry, attended, while other trail friends sent their best wishes.

The reception was a backyard bash. My fenced yard became the kids' zone with a bounce house, while Stephanie's driveway hosted a pig roast and buffet. Kegs of local Flying Bison beer chilled in the garage, and her backyard held a blues band and a big tent for the adults. Just as the food was ready, the skies opened up in a deluge. Some said rain meant good luck for marriage; if so, our "Monsoon Wedding" promised decades of happiness.

The bounce house turned into a slip-and-slide, guests crowded under tents, and the band relocated to Stephanie's living room to keep the music going. Nothing could dampen her joy; she even danced in the rain with her father. When her son worried about her soaked gown, she just laughed: "It's all right. I'm not wearing it again!"

Eventually, the rain chased most guests away, leaving only immediate family. We donated the leftover food to St. Vincent de Paul and made a lot of people happy the next day. After our relatives departed, Stephanie and I set off on our honeymoon. We chose the Berkshires, where I had left off on the AT the previous summer. Our maid of honor, Jean, had researched bed-and-breakfasts, and our friends had given us a honeymoon fund. We decided on the Birchwood Inn in Lenox, Massachusetts.

June 5, 2013 – Wednesday (Driving to the AT)

We packed the car and left by 9:30 a.m. Arriving at the Birchwood Inn, we were welcomed by Ellen, the entertaining proprietor. That afternoon, we enjoyed tea on the big front porch before walking down to the Olde Heritage Tavern for dinner. The staff, learning it was our honeymoon, bought us drinks. I chatted with a waitress about the AT and found myself inspired just talking about it. That night, we lit the fireplace in our carriage house room and read the inn's history, dating back before the Revolutionary War. It was far more formal than my trail motels, but perfect for a honeymoon.

June 6, 2013 – Thursday (Honeymoon Zero)

We thought of this as our first true honeymoon day. After a breakfast of waffles, ham, and gazpacho, we visited the Norman Rockwell Museum and had lunch in Stockbridge before returning for tea. There we met another newlywed couple from Rochester. When Ellen overheard, she surprised us with flower petals covering our bed. That evening, we kept it simple with granola bars, champagne, and plans for the days ahead. Stephanie insisted she was happy to spend her honeymoon shuttling me to trail crossings, so I could hike each day without a pack.

June 7, 2013 – Friday (Restarting the AT)

After breakfast, we checked out, and I shifted into "Hoot" mode again. Stephanie drove me back to Tyringham Road, where I'd left the trail. Naturally, it was raining … what better way to mark my return to the AT? I gave Stephanie my wedding ring for safekeeping, pulled on my poncho, and disappeared into the green, dripping woods. The trail started uphill but soon leveled, winding past Goose Pond. I didn't stop, though, as I had a new wife waiting.

Crossing the Massachusetts Turnpike felt like a milestone. Stephanie and I always pointed out the AT footbridge on drives to Cape Cod, and now I was walking across it. After about 10 wet miles, I met Stephanie at Tyne Road. We stayed in Lee that night and enjoyed dinner at Jae's Asian Bistro, wishing Buffalo had one just like it.

June 8, 2013 – Saturday

It was Stephanie's birthday, and though I felt guilty hiking, she reassured me, it was OK to continue. After breakfast, I hit the trail by 8 a.m., planning 15 miles. The climb up October Mountain Ridge was easier than I expected.

It didn't rain, but the trail itself ran like a stream, with water dripping from every branch. By 3 p.m. I reached Grange Hill Road, wet but in good spirits. I stopped there, cleaned up, and took Stephanie out for a fancy Italian dinner to celebrate her birthday.

June 9, 2013 – Sunday

We breakfasted quickly at the motel before Stephanie dropped me off again. The goal was Cheshire, 13 miles away. Hurricane Andrea was pushing up the coast, so I savored the dry weather. I climbed Crystal Mountain, descended into Dalton, and briefly lost the trail by a waterfall before finding it again. Lunch at Gore Pond restored me. Later, in Cheshire, a homeowner flagged me down because there was a young bear eating birdseed in his yard right by the trail. He offered me a ride around, but I refused. When the bear wandered too close to his wife, I banged my hiking poles to scare it off, and it bolted.

A mile later, Stephanie picked me up. At the motel, I scrubbed trail grime off more carefully than ever. It turns out, hiking as a newlywed made me self-conscious in a way I'd never been before. That night, we ate at a diner, then ended the day with a tick check. Romantic in its own way.

June 10, 2013 – Monday

Stephanie and I had breakfast at the local Moonlight Diner, and enjoyed its 50's décor as much as we enjoyed our meal. But she still had me back on the trail at my usual time, just past 8 a.m. This was the first real challenge of this stretch of the AT—Mount Greylock, the highest peak in Massachusetts, along with a few subsidiary peaks.

I reached the summit of Greylock by 11 a.m., pleasantly surprised that either the climb was easier than expected, or I was getting into better shape. Unfortunately, it was raining and I saw none of the famed views, just gray fog, drizzle, and trees. At one point, I did catch a glimpse of a small pond, and later the wind began to pick up. The observation tower was closed, so I snapped a few misty photos of it from below, rested briefly near the parking lot, then pressed on. Passing a handful of day-hikers, I noticed with some satisfaction that I was moving at a much faster pace.

The descent down a ski slope was steep, but the trail leveled out soon after. I took a fall when a tree root tripped me, but otherwise made good time, even in the rain. From William Mountain, the descent grew sharper until it felt like I was walking straight down. As hard as it was for me hiking north, I pitied the SOBO hikers who would have to climb it.

Rain always pushed me along faster, with nothing to see but the ground in front of me, so I finished the planned 14 miles quickly. The downside was an ache in my lower back I couldn't explain, especially since I wasn't even carrying a full pack. I reached the rendezvous point in North Adams by early afternoon and called Stephanie to pick me up.

When she arrived, she admitted she wasn't feeling well. We spent the afternoon resting in the motel, leaving only for a quick dinner at Olympic Pizza. I worried about her. She wasn't usually sick. I also found my motivation slipping. Marriage had shifted my focus, and with the backache not easing up, doubts crept back in.

June 11, 2013 – Tuesday

Today was my first long mileage day: 18 miles from North Adams, MA to Bennington, VT, with no road crossings in between. Stephanie dropped me off earlier than usual before heading north to find us a hotel. I entered the woods in steady rain.

The trail climbed through a private yard, following an overflowing stream for half a mile. Not long after, I crossed into Vermont, my twelfth state. Along the way, I picked up a pair of sandals someone had dropped and returned them to a grateful hiker at the next shelter.

The reason for Vermont's infamous nickname "Ver-mud" was immediately clear. The trail was waterlogged, and at one stretch I walked below a massive beaver dam where the water on the other side was at eye level. The path crossed old roads before a steep descent down Harmon Hill brought me to Route 9, where Stephanie was waiting in a downpour. I had covered 18.4 miles in 8.5 hours, which was solid time given the mud and rain.

That night at the Paradise Hotel in Bennington, we planned a Zero for the next day. The trail ahead didn't allow for slack-packing or nightly meetups, so I'd be camping again, and Stephanie would return to Buffalo. We wanted one last "honeymoon" day.

June 12, 2013 – Wednesday (Zero)

The Zero turned out to be the right choice. My joints were stiff, and I welcomed the rest. We had breakfast at the Brown Cow, lunch at the Belly Deli, and I prepped my gear while noticing Stephanie's quiet mood, which I knew was a sure sign she was holding back emotions about leaving. I felt the same conflict: the drive to finish the AT versus the pull to stay and build our life together.

That night at Madison Brewing Company, we had dinner and beer, then back at the hotel, Stephanie shaved my head while keeping up a cheerful chatter. She told me she was proud of me for committing to the hike, though I couldn't match her enthusiasm. Later, as we clung to each other in silence before sleep, I realized how torn I truly was.

June 13, 2013 – Thursday

I barely slept. We had breakfast at the Blue Benn Diner, which served real comfort food in a place packed with truckers and utility workers, always a good sign. Stephanie dropped me off and lingered in town until I could check in after 10 miles.

The return to a full pack was rough. The climb was steep, the rain relentless, and my pace slowed to two miles per hour. I reached Goddard Shelter by lunch, cold and wet, and sent Stephanie a text before she began her drive back to Buffalo.

The hike from there to Kid Gore Shelter was tough with the rain, wind, and shooting pains in my lower back that didn't feel like muscle soreness. Something was wrong, though I didn't know what. By evening, I was shivering in my bag inside a drafty old shelter, sharing the space with one other hiker who, like me, barely moved. I forced down a tasteless dinner and crawled back into the bag. By 6:30 p.m. I was already trying to sleep.

June 14, 2013 – Friday

After a miserable night, I set out early just to warm up. At Story Spring Shelter, I ate oatmeal and called Stephanie. My heart was no longer in the trail, *it was with her.* She had just arrived in Buffalo after the two-day drive, but didn't hesitate when I suggested quitting. She offered to drive back, though it would take her until the following day. We set a rendezvous at Manchester Center.

The call gave me a burst of energy. Despite pain and fatigue, I pushed up Stratton Mountain. At the summit stood a fire tower. I had always feared climbing those open structures.

One flight at a time, I forced myself up and finally made it to the top. The view was spectacular, worth the effort even though the photos didn't turn out. I understood why Benton MacKaye conceived the AT here.

Later, I met Kirk, a psychology student, and we hiked to Stratton Pond Shelter. It was packed with hikers, including Birdlady, Spiderwoman, Plantman, and others.

The conversations were lively, but my pain kept me distracted. I turned in early, realizing that the rain had finally stopped, which always seemed to happen when I was ready to quit.

June 15, 2013 – Saturday

I was up early and ready to go by 6:30 a.m., as was Plantman. We decided to walk together to Highway 11/30. I offered him a ride to Manchester Center, if he was willing to wait for Stephanie to pick us up, and he accepted the offer. Plantman was a software engineer from Poughkeepsie, NY, and a nice guy to walk and talk with. It was the best weather I had yet seen on the trail this year, and we made great time. The path was drier than it had been, and the trail here had a lot of downhill runs. At one point, we were walking along an overgrown old road and saw a moose. It is surprising how quickly such a large, 7-foot-tall animal can disappear into the woods!

Meanwhile, Stephanie drove as far as she could the night before and arrived in Manchester early. She decided to surprise me by walking up the trail. When I finally saw her ahead on a rock, I felt like I was seeing a miracle. Our joy was palpable as we clung together like we would never let go.

We all hiked out to the highway and Stephanie's car. Stephanie drove us into town and bought lunch (Plantman was a vegan, she learned, thus the apt trail name). It was her way of providing a little trail magic for Plantman. The three of us hung out for a while, talking and exchanging contact information, before dropping Plantman in town to resupply. I got in the driver's seat and headed the car back to Buffalo.

Then it was over. I drove us straight home to Buffalo, stopping only for dinner at the Buffalo Brew Pub. Over the next few days, doubts surfaced. I wondered, *had I quit too soon?* I had completed 1,650 miles, three-quarters of the AT. I thought, *surely I could have managed the last 600.* But every time I looked at my wife, or stood up with aching knees, I knew I'd made the right choice.

"New wife, new life, I don't need this strife," I told myself. I'd finish the AT someday. For now, I had to accept being a section hiker, still holding onto the dream of standing atop Katahdin.

Chapter 9

Hoot's Back

Vermont

June 2, 2014 – Monday

My first day back on the Appalachian Trail! Stephanie and I had just celebrated our first anniversary with a weekend getaway to Vermont. We stayed at the Inn at the Long Trail, a cozy spot just off the AT, though a bit farther along than where I had left off last year. To get in "the mood" for the trail, I did a little day-hike on Sunday along a loop that passed near the Inn. I knew I'd bypass that stretch later when I came through with a full pack, but for now it helped me shake the rust off. I planned to spend another night at the Inn once I reached it on the trail.

We had breakfast together at the Inn that morning, then packed up the car. Stephanie drove me out to Route 30/11 near Manchester Center, the exact spot where I'd stopped the year before. After some long hugs and kisses goodbye, I turned toward the thick woods and stepped back onto the trail.

I breathed deep, enjoying the scent of the pine trees. It was a perfect day for hiking. Still, I couldn't shake a twinge of sadness. Walking away from Stephanie always felt wrong, even if it was to complete the hike I started. Her smile as I left was warm but tight; I knew she felt the same mix of sadness and ambivalence at our temporary separation. We were committed, though, to this dream of me completing the AT, and tenaciously kept moving that dream forward regardless of our wish to be together.

Our first year of marriage had been eventful. We'd welcomed two new grandchildren: Eleanor, born to Stephanie's son Bryan in August, and Eamonn, born to my son Jarrod just three weeks later. That brought our growing family to five grandsons, one granddaughter, and two step-grandkids.

Looking back, I was grateful I had taken the year off to rest my body, enjoy our family, and start our marriage without the long separations. But I was excited to be back on the trail and planned to make it all the way to Maine this season, finally.

The trail welcomed me with a climb up to the Bromley Mountain ski area. The view stretched far but lay under a hazy sky. As I dropped down toward Mad Tom Notch, I was relieved to find my body cooperating. My legs remembered the rhythm, and soon I settled into a steady pace.

The next challenge was Styles Peak and the long pull up to Peru Peak. About halfway up, though, I hit a wall. My lungs burned, my legs felt heavy. Stephanie had warned me to take frequent breaks, and I realized, ruefully, that I'd ignored her completely. My mind had clicked back into "trail mode," but my body had other ideas. A Buffalo winter of walking and exercise couldn't prepare me for this. Lesson relearned: there's no training like the AT itself. I slowed down, took breaks, and reminded myself that a slow hike was far better than no hike at all.

The top was thick with pine and hardwoods, the ground littered with moose droppings, though no moose in sight, much to my disappointment. I reached Peru Peak Shelter after just over ten miles and decided to stop for the day. Normally, I liked camping low so climbs came in the morning, but this time it felt smart to ease myself back in.

The shelter sat in a lovely spot near a stream. The weather was cool but clear. I had the place to myself until about six, when another hiker, Sundance, showed up. He was from Pittsburgh, doing the trail in short sections. We swapped stories until hiker midnight, when we turned in, only to be woken by two loud, flashlight-wielding latecomers. They stomped around and chatted as if we weren't already asleep. Trail etiquette? Not their strong suit.

June 3, 2014 – Tuesday

In the morning, I met the culprits: iPad and Big Daddy, both from North Carolina. They were heading in the same direction, so I figured we'd be seeing more of each other. I was out before 6:30 a.m., my usual habit. The weather was perfect and the trail flat for the first stretch, so I made a solid two miles an hour until the climb up Baker Peak. The rocks there were jagged and rough, forcing me to slow down. I paused to snap pictures of a marble mine, a black hole in the hillside, and later, when I crossed Route 7, to mark my progress.

By lunchtime, I reached Little Rock Pond. Along the way, I saw a poor black-and-white dog, his muzzle full of porcupine quills. I tried to help, but he wouldn't let me get close and bolted into the woods. I hated leaving him like that.

After lunch, my energy drained away, and the last five miles were a grind. I finally staggered into Greenwall Shelter around 3:30 p.m., after nine hours on the move. A hiker named Ike was already there, and later Sundance, Big Daddy, and iPad all rolled in. At dinner, we compared notes; several had also seen the wounded dog. Clouds gathered, and by 6 p.m., the rain had set in hard. It turned into a long, wet night.

June 4, 2014 – Wednesday

The rain tapered off around four, but the forest still wept water from every branch. I set out at 6:30 a.m., my boots sinking into the mud as I climbed toward White Rocks Recreation Area and yet another Bear Mountain. From there, the path leveled out at Minerva Hinchey Shelter. I was out of water and dismayed to find none there. So I kept moving, thirsty, until Clarendon Shelter, where I finally filled up. Nearby, I got pictures of the gorge and the steep, dramatic cliffs with water far below.

The AT crossed Route 103 with rock scrambles on either side. Previous hikers had stacked flat stones into neat piles called cairns, like a spontaneous sculpture garden. I took a photo, along with another of the small airport visible from the ridge.

The rain had swollen the brooks, and soon my boots were soaked from fording streams. A washed-out bridge forced a detour onto back roads, and later I picked my way across a footbridge slung forty feet above a raging stream. The incline was steady but manageable, and I realized with some relief that I was beginning to find my "trail legs."

By late afternoon, I reached Governor Clement Shelter, where three others were already settled: Ching and Justin, a couple hiking the Long Trail, and Yolo from Germany. I expected Sundance, but he never appeared. Later, I learned he'd chosen to camp in the woods instead.

June 5, 2014 – Thursday

I was up and out by 6:00 a.m., though Yolo had already left a half hour earlier. It felt strange not to be the first one on the trail. Usually, I was the one breaking through the spider webs strung across the path overnight and shaking the water off the overhanging branches. For once, someone else had "point." It was a small luxury.

The morning started with a four-mile climb up the narrow, damp trail on Killington Peak, which was a constant series of ups and downs that wore on me quickly. It took almost three hours to reach the summit shelter, thanks to the endless rocks and roots. At the top, I found a pine forest where I'd been expecting a view. I'd imagined breaking out onto a ski slope with wide open skies, but instead I was greeted by trees and disappointment. Cooper Lodge itself was filthy, littered with empty bottles and trash. Clearly a party spot for locals. It disgusted me.

At least the weather held. It was overcast, and cool, but no rain. Perfect hiking weather, really. But as I descended the long downhill toward Route 4, my knees started to throb badly. I knew the Inn at the Long Trail was ahead, and there was even a shortcut trail that was calling my name, but I'd made a commitment to hike every single mile of the AT. I wasn't about to break that promise now. A local slowed down to offer me a ride up the hill. Tempting, but no. I trudged the last half mile, arriving at the Inn by 1:00 p.m., completely spent. I'd "hit the wall."

After a shower and laundry, I called Stephanie. I told her about my aching knees, about the simple little room I'd taken compared to the nicer one we had enjoyed together just a few days earlier. Talking to her, I realized I still didn't have that fire—the driving commitment—to finish this trail. I looked out the window at the misty, rain-soaked mountains and wondered: was it going to rain like this forever? I missed her. I was in pain. And in the back of my mind, the old doubts stirred: maybe I'd waited too long. Maybe I was too old for this.

That night I had dinner and a Guinness at the bar. To my surprise, Sundance was there, also taking a break at the Inn. He admitted he was struggling, too, and we talked about slowing down, maybe taking more rest days. I still wasn't sure I wanted to continue. Back in my room, I tried to distract myself with a book, but the pain in my knees and feet made sleep restless.

June 6, 2014 – Friday

Rain fell all night. I was thankful for four walls and a dry bed. Breakfast at the Inn came with the stay, and I met Sundance there. We planned to meet up later at Stony Brook Shelter. For me, it would be an easy eight miles, shorter than usual since I had already day-hiked part of the section the week before. I didn't leave until 8:30 a.m.

The trail started easily, winding through Gifford Woods State Park and past Thundering Falls. Then came the climb up Quimby Mountain, full of false summits, each one tricking me into thinking I was at the top, only to reveal more uphill. I saw plenty of moose droppings again, though no moose. By 1:30 p.m. I reached the shelter. If I hadn't promised Sundance, I might have pushed on, but stopping was probably wise. I read through the shelter's logbook, laughing at some of last year's entries.

Sundance didn't arrive until 4:30 p.m. He'd taken cover during an afternoon rain shower. That evening, we reminisced about hikers we'd met in 2012 like Mouse, Phoenix, Spidderman, Blue, August, and the Dutchman. It felt like a small world out here. He turned in early, but I stayed awake a while, thinking about Stephanie. This spot was close to the waterfall we had visited just last week for our anniversary. I was glad for the short day as my body felt rested, and when I finally drifted off, I slept well.

June 7, 2014 – Saturday

I wished Sundance a cheerful "good morning," but he bolted outside and threw up. He came back looking pale, blaming something he'd eaten. I worried about him, but he insisted he'd be fine.

I started out toward Bull Hill, stopping for water before the climb. The trail rolled up and down over a series of hills. For the first five miles, my body held up, then my knees started to ache again. I took aspirin to keep it manageable. The last stretch flattened out on the approach to Wintturi Shelter, and I arrived about 1:30 p.m. My knees and feet still hurt, but my promise to wait for Sundance kept me there. Probably for the best.

I poked around the woods, which were beautiful but thick with bugs. Sundance dragged in around 3:00 p.m., still sick, now with diarrhea. He alternated between his sleeping bag and the outhouse, and I was concerned. That evening, two new hikers arrived: Cishu, a retired army officer now at Lockheed Martin, and Swade, an investment advisor from England who was a huge Queen's Park Rangers fan. We talked soccer until he found out I liked Manchester United. That ended things quickly. Poor Sundance barely joined in.

June 8, 2014 – Sunday

We all woke early, but I was still the first one out of the shelter. The day began with a sweet downhill cruise to Route 12, but then the trail turned punishing. Steep ups and downs that tortured my knees. The markings were poor too on the half trail, half old-forest roads.

Midday, I found a signal and called Stephanie to wish her a happy birthday. We talked for a while, which lifted my spirits, but once I hung up, the miles dragged. By the time I reached Thistle Hill Shelter at 3:00 p.m., after 11.5 miles, I was exhausted and hurting. I called Stephanie again, this time confessing that I might come home. My knees were in constant pain. Was it lingering from Lyme disease? Or was I just old and weak?

Sundance arrived around 4:00 p.m., looking no better, and soon after, a couple of thru-hikers stopped by: Jack Rabbit and Juke Box, both government workers from Virginia who were now headed to grad school in North Carolina. They had no home for the summer, so the AT was their home. I admired that.

That evening, Sundance and I pored over the maps. His plan had always been to leave the trail in Hanover, and I finally admitted I would too. My knees were screaming. We agreed we'd both get cleaned up, rest, and maybe return next year to tackle the Presidentials together.

June 9, 2014 – Monday

I had finally made up my mind to get off the trail, though it had only been a week, and my mood was lighter because of it. I got up early, fueled myself with aspirin, and was on the trail by 6:00 a.m. Like the day before, there were plenty of ups and downs, but I reached Route 14 around 9:00 a.m.

As I crossed a bridge, I heard a bell ringing. A woman stood on her front porch, waving me over. She offered me breakfast and coffee. I had already eaten my usual oatmeal packets back at the shelter, so I declined the food but gladly accepted the coffee and sat with her for a while. She told me about her family and how they had lost their home in the flooding from Hurricane Irene back in 2011, when the river rose high enough to sweep away most of the houses near the bridge. Even three years later, the damage was still visible. The bridge I had just crossed was brand new, rebuilt after the storm. With the local store closed since the flood, her family had started feeding hikers instead. Her children were curious about us, and I thanked her for her kindness before heading back into the woods, feeling grateful that people like her existed.

From there, I climbed Griggs Mountain, the trail a constant roller coaster. All day, I leapfrogged with Jack Rabbit and Jukebox. By the time I reached Norwich, Vermont, which was the last town before New Hampshire, I found them on Elm Street beside a cooler of trail magic.

We dug into the watermelon just as the homeowner came out to greet us. She introduced herself by her trail name, Short-and-Sweet, and told us she and her husband, Graybeard, hosted hikers regularly. She offered us a shower, laundry, and a place to sleep. I told her Sundance would be along soon, and when he arrived, he was welcomed too.

After cleaning up, Sundance and I borrowed some spare clothes and walked down the hill into Hanover, New Hampshire. We grabbed burgers and beers, and I picked up a book for the long bus ride home. Hanover's free bus service, courtesy of Dartmouth College and the town, made it easy to get around. On our way back, Graybeard spotted us and drove us up the hill.

That night, Short-and-Sweet told us why they opened their home. Years earlier, their son had been hiking in the Smokies when he ignored an Achilles tendon injury that became infected. A local man gave him and his buddy a ride to the hospital and then hosted them for an entire week while he recovered. When the grateful parents tried to repay him, he refused and told them to "pay it forward." They had been doing just that ever since.

They set up air mattresses in their finished basement, and the four of us hikers enjoyed the warmth and comfort. I should have slept soundly, but I didn't. Doubts crept back in, whispering that maybe I should keep going. But my aching knees and returning foot pain reminded me why I had decided to leave the trail this year.

June 10, 2014 – Tuesday

We woke at 6:00 a.m., and Graybeard drove us to the bus stop in Hanover. The ride to Boston took about three hours. From there, Sundance would head to Pittsburgh while I went west to Buffalo.

On the bus, a black-and-white movie, *Young Abe Lincoln*, helped pass the time. At the Boston terminal, Sundance and I said our goodbyes, promising to talk about hiking together next year. After lunch, I boarded the Greyhound for Buffalo.

The ride was long, with endless stops, and I had plenty of time to think about my future. My knees and foot would need medical attention, and whether I could return to the AT depended on what the doctors said. I hoped I could hike with Sundance again if I did. Hiking alone had been difficult and lonely at times.

It was nearly 11:00 p.m. when we finally pulled into Buffalo. Stephanie and Nathan, who had moved back to the area, were waiting, ready to take me to the new home Stephanie and I had bought after our wedding last year. As tired as I was, it felt good to be home.

Chapter 10

Presidential Mountains

New Hampshire

June 3, 2015 – Wednesday

What a day! It started at 4:15 a.m. at my house in Buffalo, where I ate, dressed, and then heaved my pack into the car so Stephanie could drive me to the airport for a 6:25 a.m. JetBlue flight to Boston. The plan was for Sundance and me to both fly into Boston from our respective cities in time to catch the bus to Hanover, NH and start our hike that very day, planning to get to Moose Mountain Shelter.

Landing early, I had plenty of time to find the bus stop in Terminal C and board the bus to Hanover, NH. I was annoyed that the airline had managed to lose one of my two heavy-duty water bottles. Since I had to sterilize and carry all my drinking water, I'd have to replace the water bottle before hiking. However, since I couldn't bring the small propane canister for my stove on the airplane, I was already planning to find an outfitter in Hanover, so I didn't anticipate a major problem. When I boarded the bus, I was glad to see Sundance already on it, since the bus had stopped at his terminal first.

I felt confident as the bus drove north. Although I had my usual fears and reservations, I was determined to overcome them. I felt I was in far better shape than the previous year, having worked out intensely all winter. My knees had been diagnosed with severe arthritis, with bone rubbing on bone, which explained the constant pain. However, I had received an injection into the knee joints that seemed to decrease the pain. (This was after convincing the shocked orthopedic doctor that I wasn't looking for knee replacement surgery, I just wanted to finish hiking the AT.) I chuckled, remembering how the surgeon couldn't believe this gray-haired old man with terrible knee x-rays wasn't lying on a couch all day.

The bus arrived in Hanover at noon, and I set out to find an outfitter. I discovered that the propane canister that fit my stove wasn't readily available. There was only one outfitter in town, Zimmerman's, and they were out of it, although they were expecting a shipment later in the day. Not wanting to waste time, I tried to find it at other locations around town with no luck. Sundance ate dried food and didn't even carry a stove, but he was willing to wait for me to get what I needed. Returning to Zimmerman's, I was lucky to arrive just as the shipment came in, and I purchased the propane canister and the replacement water bottle. We filled our bottles at the local community center (a luxury to have clean drinking water that we didn't first need to sterilize) and headed out onto the trail much later than planned.

Despite working out at the gym every day over the winter, including a half hour on the stairclimber (80 "floors") to keep in shape, I soon realized that I had once again underestimated the physical demands of the AT. It was just over 11 miles to our planned shelter. We had walked all over town trying to find the propane canister, and we weren't starting out fresh. At least the weather was nice. By the time we arrived at the shelter, I was completely spent. The food I made for dinner tasted terrible for some reason, and I hurt all over. We both decided to hit the sack by 8:00 p.m.

June 4, 2015 – Thursday

I got up and out by 6:20 a.m., quickly falling back into my hiker habits. After all, this was my fourth year on the AT. We only planned a hike of 12.4 miles, but it was very difficult terrain. There were two big climbs, including Smarts Mountain, which came as a surprise. I had forgotten to pack the map for this first section, so I didn't know what to expect. The AT map set that Stephanie had purchased for me so long ago included very accurate terrain maps, and typically, I would pore over the maps at night to plan my next day's hike. Not knowing what to expect seemed to make it worse, and I found the hills very challenging.

I started out alone, as usual, but Sundance caught up with me at Trapper John Shelter at midday. Good thing, because I was getting depressed and having thoughts of quitting already, and the company helped take my mind off things. We met three other section hikers. There was an older couple with trail names Lifeguard and Serendipity, who were using two vehicles to slack pack each section road-to-road. The third hiker was a very sweet young lady named Acorn, who was hiking southbound from NH to NY. She strongly reminded me of my daughter-in-law Colleen in manner, though they didn't look at all alike.

Sundance and I were still hiking together when we came upon trail magic outside the house of a college professor named Bill. Although he wasn't there, he left access to a water spigot and a refrigerator with ice cream (heaven!). That's where we met Acorn again, who was writing her blog because the house also had wi-fi available. We later discovered that Bill let hikers camp on his property.

Continuing on, Sundance pulled ahead as we started our climb up Smarts Mt. Apparently, he spooked a bear without seeing it, but the bear came running down the trail right toward me. Instinctively, I raised my hiking poles in the air, yelling, "there's a bear!" The bear veered off into the woods upon hearing me. Sundance heard me yelling, but later told me he thought I was just hollering to psych myself up for the climb.

We made it to the top of the mountain and camped, making plans for the next day. Sundance preferred being alone in a tent, but I stayed in the Firewarden's Cabin, preferring shelters to tents when available. It was a rundown-looking place, but it was solid and had no mice, and I had the place to myself, except for a tick that I found crawling on me. I set up my sleeping bag on a bench inside, because the floor was wavy and uneven. I heard something creeping around outside at night, but I was safe in the cabin.

I took ibuprofen that night, but I still hurt all over. I was so discouraged! I thought I had worked out enough to remain in hiking shape, and the knee injections had noticeably helped when I was home. The rigors of the trail were just significantly harder than any other exercise, and my body let me know it. I knew that these mountains were considered the hardest part of the entire AT, and I thought I was mentally and physically prepared. Instead, I felt really drained. At least I could get a cell signal from the mountain top, so I got to talk to Stephanie, who always cheered me up and encouraged me.

June 5, 2015 – Friday

I was up and out early, hiking alone most of the day. The first four miles were downhill off Smarts Mountain, and I made good time. Then came Mt. Cube, which forced me into hand-over-hand rock climbing with my hiking poles strapped to my pack. Climbing rock faces with a full pack was no fun. At the time, it felt like the toughest challenge I'd faced so far, though later I'd look back on it as relatively easy. The steep descent that followed was better, though still tricky with the weight on my back.

On the way down, I ran into Lifeguard and Serendipity slack-packing southbound. I envied them but was surprised to realize I actually felt pretty good.

After Mt. Cube, the trail rolled up and down until I reached the Ore Hill tent site. The old shelter there had burned down in 2011, but the flat ground made for a decent campsite. I pitched my tent under the trees just as Sundance showed up. Soon after, three thru-hikers passed through: Sycamore from Michigan, and Little Debbie and Deadline from Massachusetts. They'd started February 28th at Springer Mountain and planned to finish the entire AT by the end of June so Deadline could get married, hence his trail name. They only stopped for a quick snack before pushing on into the darkening sky.

Not long after, the rain started. I thought of them out there in the wet while I stayed mostly dry beneath the trees. I settled into my tent, reviewing the day with a smile. No bears, and a rock climb I'd managed without issue. Maybe I could really do this after all.

June 6, 2015 – Saturday

Today was easier, just 7½ miles down to Route 25, where Sundance and I headed for the Hiker's Welcome Hostel in Glencliff. It was run by a former thru-hiker named Legion.

The hostel was rustic, to say the least. Showers, laundry, and toilets were outside. The floors were stone, and the hot water took forever to heat. I claimed a bunk, but Sundance decided to tent it. He blamed the bugs in the bunkhouse, and there were plenty of them—dead sandflies and moths littered the mattress I brushed off before laying out my sleeping bag. To me, it wasn't much different from a shelter, and at least the mattress was softer than my pad. I figured Sundance just liked being alone, and with the hostel filling up fast, I couldn't blame him.

I showered, did laundry, and called Stephanie to check in. By afternoon, more hikers started rolling in. Sycamore and Deadline returned from slack-packing Mt. Moosilauke. Legion offered a shuttle to the north end of the mountain so hikers could slack-pack southbound and spend a second night at the hostel. Sundance and I decided to take him up on it.

Later, two flip-floppers arrived: Ghost Chili, from Australia, and Smiles, from Michigan. Both were hiking barefoot. Smiles was tall, always smiling, and it was obvious where she got her trail name. Ghost Chili was taller still, with long hair and a wild beard. They'd met on the trail and become a pair.

Then came Mango and Sunrise, an older couple from New York City. Sunrise was of Asian descent, Mango had a scholarly look with his gray beard, and both were easygoing and kind. Finally, a father-son team, Rammer Jammer and Little Foot, filled the place even more.

The day turned lively with hikers everywhere, trading stories and heading into town for food. I stayed back to eat from my own pack and lighten my load. I did wander out to hunt for Steripen batteries, but came up empty. Back at the hostel, I settled in with the others, swapping trail tales while Dodger and Rocky, a pair of weekend hikers, showed up to round out the crowd.

By evening, the place buzzed with energy. Most of us planned to slack-pack Moosilauke the next day, so it felt like a reunion waiting to happen.

June 7, 2015 – Sunday

I "slept in" until 5:30 a.m., since I didn't need to pack up after breakfast for the hike. Legion made breakfast for everyone at the hostel, then shuttled me, Sundance, Rocky, Dodger, Sunrise, and Mango up to Kinsman Notch for the day's slack-packing hike south back to the hostel. On the way, we passed a moose by the side of the road. At the trailhead, we chatted, snapped pictures, and then set off.

The initial climb was steep and ran next to Beaver Brook Cascade for about a mile and a half, alongside a series of waterfalls, followed by a slow and steady incline to the top. Once above the tree line, we were treated to a tremendous 360-degree view from the summit. The day was perfect; clear, beautiful, exhilarating, and we lingered there soaking it all in while the whole hostel slack-pack crew eventually gathered. Lifeguard and Serendipity joined us for a while, and I enjoyed the feeling of camaraderie. Normally, I hiked alone, only meeting up with Sundance at a predetermined spot each evening, so having a group connection like this felt invigorating.

The descent toward Route 25 was a difficult four miles of steep downhill over scattered rocks, followed by three miles of relatively flat terrain. I gradually pulled ahead of Sundance but stopped and waited for him at Jeffers Brook, a stream at the highway that we had to ford. I unzipped the bottom half of my hiker pants, swapped my boots for water shoes, and stepped into the knee-deep stream. The icy water, fed by mountain snowmelt, bit into my legs but felt wonderful on my aching feet.

Returning to the hostel after the slack-pack was a relief, but I was unhappy to notice that my back hurt and my left foot throbbed. Even with some Vitamin I, I felt a "world of hurt." Thankfully, the conversation with the other hikers distracted me. A new hiker, Appalachian Snail, arrived. She was an older woman, probably my age, with a story similar to mine. She too had left a job to hike the AT, but after getting injured, had to abandon her thru-hike and was now section-hiking, just like me. I was impressed to learn she'd already had a knee replacement and was still out here. Sadly, she had an ankle injury now and was leaving the trail the next day when her husband came to pick her up.

That night, Sundance stayed in his tent, leaving me and Appalachian Snail the only two hikers in the hostel. I called Stephanie for her birthday the next day, unsure if I'd have service then. I had prepared a surprise gift for her. Before leaving, I hid a card and some new pillows in the guest room, knowing how she'd been complaining about hers. I guided her to the room over the phone, and she was surprised and touched. I smiled at how perfectly it had worked out, even from the trail.

June 8, 2015 – Monday

Part of the slack-packing deal was that Legion would return us to Kinsman Notch after our second night at the hostel, this time with our full packs to continue north. After a hot breakfast, the shuttle dropped us at 7:20 a.m. into light rain and a trail choked with fog and mist, which worsened as we climbed Mt. Wolf and then the twin peaks of South and North Kinsman.

It was a grueling day, full of hand-over-hand climbs. Mt. Wolf was rocky, but mercifully short. Still, it took us over 5½ hours to cover just 7.5 miles to Eliza Brook Shelter for lunch. Afterward came a punishing, steep, rocky climb peppered with false summits. Time after time, I thought we had reached the top, like climbing stairs to a landing, only to discover the trail turning upward again. The descents were no easier: just as steep, just as rocky, and just as punishing. We finally reached Kinsman Pond Shelter around 5:15 p.m., having managed only 11.5 miles all day. It was disheartening, especially since the mist and fog robbed us of any views that might have made the suffering worthwhile.

The shelter itself was unusual, with four walls and a small entrance opening, unlike the typical three-sided style. Later, another thru-hiker, Lunchbox, arrived. He was from California and had already completed the Pacific Crest Trail.

He was planning to finish the AT and then tackle the Continental Divide Trail. We talked about the different long trails for a while, which was fascinating.

Kinsman Pond was nearby, but when I walked down to see it, dense fog rose from the water, and I couldn't see a thing—not even the surface. It was eerie. With the dampness in the air, I was wet despite the absence of rain. That night, after the exhausting day, we were all in our sleeping bags by 8:00 p.m., grateful for warmth against the surprising cold.

June 9, 2015 – Tuesday

I woke to gray skies after a rainy night, packed up, and was on the trail by 6:30 a.m.

It took me two full hours to cover just two miles to Lonesome Lake Hut, managed by the Appalachian Mountain Club (AMC). The staff, called the "Croo," ran the place. I asked about water and the weather forecast. They told me thunderstorms were expected on Franconia Ridge and strongly advised against attempting the ridge in that weather. They also warned that the bridge at Cascade Creek was gone and suggested an alternate route to Franconia Notch.

I waited for Sundance to arrive to talk it over. When he did, the Croo member ignored him completely, which struck me as rude, but I figured it was because we weren't paying customers. Luckily, another Croo member named Sam came in and offered to guide us to the alternate route. He gave us plenty of details, including where to find lodging to avoid the incoming storms.

We reached Lafayette Campground after slow, wet hiking and found information about Indian Head Resort. The campground attendant even called and reserved us a room. It required a four-mile detour, but by then we were drenched to our underwear anyway. It felt more like swimming than hiking. The rain was so heavy I nearly missed a blaze and turned wrong, but Sundance caught it. Between the storm and the detour, we only covered 4.7 trail miles, though we walked closer to 8 total.

The resort, in the off-season, gave us a hiker discount, and the expense wasn't as bad as we feared. We showered, did laundry, and enjoyed the luxury of a real room with a view of the Presidential range, though at the time, I didn't realize we'd be climbing those very peaks next. I called Stephanie in the afternoon and again at bedtime, happy to have service. Later, Sundance went into town for food and beer, and I watched

Women's World Cup soccer on TV before drifting off, warm and comfortable, as thunderstorms raged outside.

June 10, 2015 – Wednesday

The resort shuttle dropped us back at the trailhead around 7:30 a.m.

That spared us the four-mile walk back, though we still had to hike about a mile to rejoin the AT where we'd left it. The initial climb was steep but well-worn, and once on Franconia Ridge, the views were breathtaking. The storms had cleared, leaving us above the trees with sweeping panoramas. The walk from Liberty Mt. to Mt. Lafayette was rocky and full of ups and downs, but being able to see the trail stretch ahead all the way to Garfield made it exhilarating. I took picture after picture, even knowing none could capture the grandeur of the place.

But once we began descending Lafayette, the magic faded. The trail became even rockier, and Garfield was worse. I fell hard on one descent. Instinctively, I turned to land on my back, avoiding injury, but the scare rattled me. A slip like that could easily have broken a wrist or ankle. With the trail as wet as it was, much of it felt like walking down a waterfall. I slowed, moving cautiously, my hiking poles probing each step. My joy from earlier evaporated, replaced by nerves and weariness. The Presidentials, I realized, were challenging less for their elevation than for their endless rocks and grueling trail conditions.

The day ended at Galehead Hut, just 13 miles in distance but across four major mountains and countless "bumps." Camping options here in the Presidentials were limited, so AMC huts were the only real choice. Thankfully, I had signed up for an AMC membership before my trip, and that discount helped. We arrived late, and the girl running the hut gave me a deal for my bunk and dinner. Sundance, preferring solitude as always, stealth camped nearby.

To my delight, Ghost Chili and Smiles were at the hut, two of the happiest and most positive hikers I had met. We enjoyed dinner and good conversation together, and I went to bed around 9:00 p.m.

The hut quieted at 9:30 p.m., but my knees throbbed. I lay there with a creeping worry that this was the same pain that had pulled me off the trail the year before.

June 11, 2015 – Thursday

I scored an early breakfast from the hut's cook and was on the trail by 6:30 a.m.

The morning began with a section called the Beltway. It was a steep, straight line of rocks climbing upward. I felt good, moving quickly, but my mind was already on the evening when Stephanie planned to meet me and Sundance at Crawford Notch. Distracted, I missed a trail junction and followed the wrong path toward Bond Cliffs. Two miles later, a couple stopped me and told me I was no longer on the AT. Furious at myself, I lost another hour backtracking. Determined to make up time, I started rock-hopping, pushing harder than I should have.

I reached Zealand Falls Hut around 3:00 p.m. for a quick break, then pressed on to Ethan Pond Shelter, where I expected to find Sundance. Instead, I found Ghost Chili and Smiles, but no Sundance. They hadn't seen him all day. I assumed he had pushed on to Route 302 where Stephanie was waiting. Heading down the trail again, I met two southbound hikers who confirmed that Sundance was indeed at the road. The walk was downhill, but long. I finally stumbled out of the woods around 7:30 p.m., and there they were, Stephanie and Sundance waiting for me. The moment I saw her, my cares melted away. *Oh, how I love that woman.*

Stephanie had spent the previous night in Bennington, VT, after the long drive from Buffalo, then scouted lodging near Crawford Notch while waiting for us. She had been uncertain whether she'd see us that evening or the next, but she parked at Route 302 at 3:30 p.m. as planned. As dusk fell without any sign of me, she drove a narrow access road from the parking lot and found another lot a half mile away, where Sundance was waiting. They introduced themselves and began to backtrack together in the fading light, worried that something might have happened to me.

At the railroad crossing, they met a northbound hiker named Elmer who said he'd passed me just minutes before. Sure enough, moments later, I came crunching along the gravel bed, exhausted but relieved to see them. Stephanie hugged me so tightly I could feel her relief. We piled into her car, and I explained my wrong turn and long day while she drove us to a motel.

Sundance took his own room to give us space and headed to a local bar. Stephanie took me to dinner at a place called Delaney's, and knowing I had a Zero the next day, I let myself enjoy a beer with my meal.

I rarely drank on the trail, since even one beer made hiking the next day miserable, but tonight was different. Stephanie excitedly told me she'd spotted a fisher crossing the road earlier, a rare sight. Back at the motel, she massaged my aching feet, which felt like heaven. I figured with the wrong turn I'd walked about 18 miles, an enormous day for the Whites. My legs throbbed, but eventually I drifted into sleep.

June 12, 2015 – Friday (Zero)

Today was a planned Zero, and I needed it. My knees were aching badly, and more than anything, I wanted time with Stephanie. The three of us went to a local spot called Priscilla's for a big breakfast. Later, I handled laundry while Stephanie drove Sundance to shop for new boots.

As I sat outside the motel waiting for the dryer to finish, a familiar face appeared. It was Mango! He told me he had slipped at the very same waterfall where I'd fallen and had banged up his knee. He and his wife Sunrise were looking for lodging, but this hotel was full. When Stephanie returned, she offered to drive the seventy-year-old Mango and his sixty-nine-year-old wife to another hotel. They gratefully accepted. I was reminded again what a generous and kindhearted woman I had married.

The rest of the day, I set aside "Hoot" and became Greg again, just enjoying my wife. Even after two years of marriage, I still felt like a newlywed. My spirits soared with every hour we had together. That evening, we met Sundance for Mexican food, disappointing, unfortunately, but I didn't care much because I was too happy being with Stephanie. She watched curiously as Sundance and I spread out maps and planned our next section. Later, back at the motel, I fell asleep quickly but woke at 11:30 p.m. with throbbing legs. The pain was bad enough that I had to get up for aspirin before I could drift off again. It worried me, especially after a full rest day.

June 13, 2015 – Saturday

We went back to Priscilla's for another hearty breakfast, then Stephanie drove us to Route 302 at Crawford Notch to return to the trail. Saying goodbye was hard. I missed her with every step I took away. She was driving on to drop resupply packages for me at Pinkham Notch and Gorham before returning home. It was too short a visit, but the Whites didn't allow for the kind of slack-packing she had managed for me in other states. Here, the roads were few, and the mountains were isolated.

The trail wasted no time... up we went, climbing Mt. Webster. From the road, Stephanie had looked up at the cliffs and thought them impossibly steep. She wasn't wrong. The climb took us from 1,500 feet to over 4,000 in just three miles. It was challenging but rewarding. At the top, the Webster Cliffs gave us a stunning view of Crawford Notch, and for a while, the suffering felt worthwhile.

We made steady progress to the Nauman Tent Sites near Mizpah Spring Hut, both run by the AMC. The ground was too rocky for normal camping, so wooden platforms had been built for tents. Sundance and I shared one, then went to the hut to plan. He told me he would be leaving in nine days and hoped to reach Ashford, ME, before going home.

As night fell, hikers kept arriving until the caretaker had to pack three or four tents on each platform. The place turned into a tent city. The hut was available, but at a steep price compared to the $8 tent site. We stayed put, chatting until 7:30 p.m. before crawling into our tents for sleep.

June 14, 2015 – Sunday

We were up early and on the trail by 5:50 a.m., because we knew this would be a tough day. The first task: climb Mt. Washington, at 6,288 feet. The ascent was as brutal as we expected, and the air was cold at the top. To our surprise, the summit was crowded with tourists who had driven up, which felt anticlimactic after the sweat and struggle it had taken us to get there.

I tried to call Stephanie, but the cell service was poor, so I wasn't sure how much she understood. Sundance and I stood near the observation platform where there was a live camera feed, hoping she could see us if she was watching online. We weren't sure if the signal worked.

I later learned that Stephanie was at work that morning, seeing hospitalized veterinary patients, when my special ringtone went off. She was shocked when I told her we were already on top of Mt. Washington. Frantically, she tried to log onto the observation camera feed but couldn't get through on her iPad. The clinic owner's son, working nearby, set up her connection just in time. She pulled up the live feed and saw me and Sundance standing on the observation deck, bundled against the cold but smiling at the camera. She grabbed a screenshot just in time; a memory captured despite the distance.

Leaving Mt. Washington, the trail turned miserable. Cairns marked the path across vast rock fields, but the footing was terrible with loose stones and endless ups and downs.

I lost track of Sundance and didn't see him again until Madison Spring Hut. We had planned to push on to a tent site a mile down a rocky, poor trail, but we were spent. Neither of us had the energy. We decided to stay at the hut despite the cost.

Dinner was served family-style, and the Croo introduced themselves. One young woman, Jess, mentioned she had attended the University of Buffalo. I went up afterward to chat. She hadn't met anyone else from our suburb of Amherst, and it felt nice to share a small connection to home.

But that night I felt something new and troubling: sharp, painful cramps in my calves and muscles. This wasn't the fatigue pain of Georgia or North Carolina when I was still building trail legs, it was different, nastier. I worried something was wrong, but tried to push it from my mind and eventually fell asleep.

June 15, 2015 – Monday

After a good breakfast at the hut, Sundance and I started the climb up Mt. Madison. The day was blowing misty and raw. The wind was so fierce that it actually knocked me over at one point. With both trekking poles planted firmly, I picked my way slowly across slick, wet rocks while the gale buffeted us from every side. The first two miles were an agonizing crawl across steep, rocky, and completely exposed to the elements. I prayed never to face that kind of section again.

Dropping below the treeline eased the wind, but the trail didn't get any friendlier. My knees hurt so badly that I kept stumbling, and more than once I lost my balance. One fall downhill left me so weak I had trouble getting back on my feet. Something was seriously wrong. I could feel both muscle weakness and a lack of balance on top of the pain, and it scared me.

The last mile and a half were gentler, and we eventually descended into Joe Dodge Lodge near Pinkham Notch, where Stephanie had left me a resupply box. There was nowhere else to stay, so we booked bunks in a room shared with a father-and-son pair who didn't seem thrilled to have company. Sundance suspected they had hoped to keep the room to themselves.

We showered, rested, and had dinner, but I turned in early. Sleep didn't come until I numbed the pain with a cocktail of aspirin and ibuprofen. My mattress was fine. Comfortable even. It was my body that was the problem. I wrote in my journal: *"just killing me."*

116

June 16, 2015 – Tuesday

After breakfast at the lodge, we started up into the Wildcat Range. A mile in, Sundance realized he'd forgotten his maps back at Joe Dodge and had to hike back. I pressed on. At the first summit, I got a cell signal and called Stephanie. I confessed how bad my knee pain had gotten and how much it was draining my desire to continue. I told her I was considering leaving the trail in Gorham.

On the phone, she couldn't tell if I was just worn down and discouraged or if something was really wrong. She knew I always second-guessed myself whenever I got off the AT. But she remembered seeing my pain first-hand just a few days earlier, and with sadness in her voice, she admitted it might be best to quit. I was going to finish this section and go home again to heal and recover.

The day was gray and threatening rain, with fog, and mist curling in the valleys. The trail went up and down relentlessly, more climbs than descents. At one point, I passed an old tow rope used by skiers. Though standing at the summit, I laughed at the thought of needing it. A flash of blue caught my eye: a Cerulean Warbler! A brand-new bird for my life list, and that small joy lifted my spirits.

Sundance caught up to me just as the rain began. The last Wildcat descent was insanely steep, and with Carter Notch Hut less than a mile away, we decided to call it a night. The Croo seemed less than welcoming, half-heartedly suggesting there were "great tent sites" five minutes up the trail. Soaked through, neither of us wanted to hear it. We stayed, though I never shook the sense that they resented our intrusion on what they'd hoped would be a quiet night. Dinner was fine, but the atmosphere was strained.

The layout was simple: a central lodge for meals, and small bunk cabins that slept four. At least I had a room to myself, as did Sundance, because he was always aware of his snoring. I spread my wet clothes out, hoping they'd dry a little, and crawled into bed. For once, I slept fairly well.

June 17, 2015 – Wednesday

The morning dawned cold and bright. It was perfect hiking weather. After breakfast, we started the climb up Carter Dome under bright sunshine. The air was crisp, cool, and kind to hikers.

The trail roller-coastered up and down until Zeta Pass, then dropped us sharply before climbing again into the Carters. Near North Carter Peak, the vegetation grew stunted, though we never broke treeline. I stopped to take pictures, one of them of Sundance grinning with a cigar clenched between his teeth at the summit.

Then came the worst downhill I'd yet encountered. It was so steep I often sat and slid on my backside, not trusting my feet. We reached Imp Shelter around 3:00 p.m., set up camp, and agreed on an early start for Gorham in the morning. I managed a brief call to Stephanie to confirm our plans.

That evening, two thru-hikers arrived: Bourbon and White Hawk from Tennessee. They were pushing huge miles, hoping to finish by July 10th. They recommended the White Mountain Hostel on Route 2 in Gorham. Sounded like just what we needed. By 7:30 p.m., we were all in our sleeping bags.

June 18, 2015 – Thursday

I barely slept but was up before dawn, and we hit the trail at 5:50 a.m. The day's one big climb involved long stretches of sloping rock, interspersed with short ascents and descents before a sharp drop. Thankfully, stone steps had been built into the slope, making it less treacherous than the day before.

The trail eventually mellowed into a 3½-mile gradual descent to Route 2. By noon, we reached the White Mountain Hostel, the very one Bourbon and White Hawk had recommended. It was fantastic. Just $33 got us a bunk with actual sheets (a rare treat), a shower, laundry, and breakfast. Marnie, the owner, radiated energy and genuine warmth. She cared about hikers; that much was obvious. When she heard we planned to leave the AT, she promised us a ride to the stop for the bus to Boston, where we could catch flights back to our respective homes.

Inside, I recognized Mango and Sunrise, along with Bourbon and White Hawk. We showered, washed clothes, and went into town. I picked up the supply box Stephanie had left and promptly mailed it home unopened. There was no need for it now. The rest of the day was spent lounging and trading stories.

I couldn't help noticing the irony: every time I decided to leave the AT, the weather turned beautiful, almost mocking me. It would have been a perfect hiking day. That night, we watched a documentary on the Pacific Crest Trail, swapping comparisons with our own battered Appalachian Trail legs.

June 19, 2015 – Friday (Back to Buffalo)

Marnie cooked a wonderful breakfast, making each hiker feel like family. Later, I learned she sold the hostel to one of her employees, who kept the same spirit alive.

A section hiker named Southside gave us a lift to the bus terminal. He joked that his "training" for the AT had been gaining 35 pounds and doing no walking, a plan that obviously failed, and he was headed back to Rhode Island.

The bus to Boston was uneventful, about four hours. I arrived early enough to check my pack, buy a hot pretzel, pick up a book, and wait for my 5:15 flight home via Baltimore. Everything went smoothly. When I landed in Buffalo, Stephanie was waiting. Seeing her again filled me with relief. We talked quietly on the way home before collapsing into bed.

Interlude – June 25, 2015 – Friday

After a week at home, I added an update to my journal. My legs still ached, and my right knee locked if I held it in one position too long. I knew I had made the right choice to leave.

Blue, the thru-hiker who had come to our wedding, called to congratulate me on finishing the White Mountains, saying it was the hardest part of the entire AT. That gave me some comfort.

I left the door open to trying again next year, maybe joining Sundance, but for 2015, I was done. Truth be told, the idea of finishing the AT didn't stir me much anymore. What nagged at me was the fear of letting people down, especially Stephanie, who had supported me every step of the way.

Chapter 11

End in Sight

New Hampshire / Maine

June 14, 2016 – Tuesday (Returning to the trail)

I had wrestled with the idea of completing the AT for the entire previous year. My legs hurt for months after I went home the year before, and my knees were constantly sore. Still, after much consideration, I decided to try again. I would be turning 65 later this year, and this would mark my fifth attempt to complete the AT. I wasn't sure how many more tries my body could take. I switched my training from strength work to more walking and biking, hoping it would better prepare me for the brutal northern stretch. Even so, I carried real reservations. The AT takes a toll on the body, yes—but it's also a mental battle. I wasn't sure my head was in the right place. But my stubborn streak and tenacity pushed me forward. I couldn't let go of the dream.

That morning started at home with Stephanie. After breakfast, she drove me to the airport. I breezed through security, bought a paper to pass the time, and braced myself for a day of travel—and plenty of waiting. I landed in Boston early, grabbed my pack from baggage claim, and went in search of Sundance, who was flying in from near Pittsburgh. I spotted him outside Terminal B, puffing on a cigar. We moved to the concourse between Terminals A and B, where a row of rocking chairs let us sit and watch the planes taxi in and out. Settling into those chairs, I felt the hiker mindset start to return. After a long year, Greg faded away, and I became Hoot once again.

At 3:45 p.m., we boarded the bus and immediately got stuck in Boston traffic—an hour and a half delay before we even reached open road. At least the weather was decent. The bus wound its way through small New England towns, each with its own charm. By the time we reached Gorham, NH, it was 10:30 p.m.

Marnie from the White Mountains Lodge and Hostel was waiting for us, a welcome sight after such a long haul. Once registered for the night, I called Stephanie to let her know I'd made it safely back to Gorham. Hanging up, I sat quietly on my bed, letting it sink in. Tomorrow, I'd be back on the AT.

June 15, 2016 – Wednesday

I got up at 5:30 a.m. and took a long shower, knowing it would probably be my last for a while. Over breakfast, I met some of the other travelers gathered around the family-style table: Shelob, another AT hiker; Dominique, who had pedaled all the way from Montreal; and Guardian, who had already completed the AT earlier in the year and now worked at the hostel. I chatted with Melissa, the cook, and learned she had hiked the AT the year before. I told her how much I appreciated the massive breakfast burritos.

The trail greeted us gently at first, but soon turned into a relentless grind with 2,000 feet of climbing. The first ascent up Cascade Mountain rewarded me with views of the Presidential Range we had conquered the year before. At least that was behind us. Still, I quickly remembered how much I disliked the uphills. My body struggled and, worse, my doubts came rushing back. Off-trail, I always managed to forget the pain—the amnesia that lured me back again and again. But in the moment, I wondered: Was I crazy to return to the AT?

Sundance was battling leg cramps, so our pace dropped to a crawl—barely a mile per hour. The trail seemed made of nothing but rocks, steep pitches, and water. I'd forgotten how miserable a wet trail could be. The downhills were slick, the uphills punishing. It felt as though the AT itself was conspiring to slow us down and test our resolve. By 6:00 p.m. we reached Gentian Pond Shelter, only 11.8 miles covered in about as many hours.

I called Stephanie immediately, venting about how sore and tired I was. I stopped short of saying I'd made a mistake in coming back, but she could hear the weight in my voice. She worked her magic, reminding me of the sunshine, the fresh air, and the fact that I always complained on my first day back. She even laughed, pointing out how I was once thrilled to hit 8 miles a day and now I was disappointed in 12. Her encouragement lifted me just enough. After hanging up, I cooked dinner, stretched out in my bag, and tried to rest my weary body.

June 16, 2016 – Thursday

We started early, around 6:15 a.m., under a bright, clear sky. The trail wasted no time in proving difficult. The climb up Mt. Success—which I promptly renamed Mt. Sucks A**—topped out at 3,500 feet. If the mountains had been steady ascents and descents, I could've managed. But the endless rollercoaster of rocky ups and downs drained me.

At last, we reached the New Hampshire-Maine border. Stepping into Maine felt huge; we were now in our 14th and final state. Only 281 miles left! For the first time, I could see the end of this odyssey. We didn't need to rush; just beat the snow to Baxter State Park. That thought alone gave me a surge of strength.

The boost carried me up Carlo Col and into the Goose Eye Range. Goose Eye's North Peak introduced me to rebar ladders bolted into vertical rock. With a 100-foot drop beside me, I had to shift my body awkwardly from one side to another, my pack and poles making the climb even harder. I hated heights and avoided looking down. One hiker even carried his dog up, though I couldn't fathom how. Though the views from the summit were spectacular, the climb was nerve-wracking.

Later, I stumbled across piles of lumber dropped by helicopter for puncheon boardwalk repairs, strange to see in such remote wilderness. At one point, I glanced back and saw Sundance far behind me, tiny against the vast landscape. The distance we had covered sank in, and I kept walking, tired but determined.

It was after 7:00 p.m. when we reached Full Goose Shelter, just 9.6 miles in nearly 13 hours. I was utterly spent, my body threatening to collapse with every step. I stayed in the shelter with two NOBOs, Tinder and Bryan O, while Sundance set up his tent. That night, I reflected that we weren't really hiking together—we just happened to be moving through the same mountains. My hike had always been a solitary one, with companions drifting in and out. Plus-Two had been the closest to a real partner, and I cherished the memory of our shared miles. He had promised to meet me in Maine, near where he lived, when I finally made it. Others—Blue, Steve-O, Mouse, Rainbow—remained connected through social media, cheering me on from afar. Even when I felt alone, I knew they were with me in spirit.

June 17, 2016 – Friday

We started late for us, around 7:00 a.m., with only five miles planned. But those five miles loomed: Mahoosuc Notch and Mahoosuc Arm, infamous as the toughest mile on the AT. First, we had to get up and down Fulling Mill Mountain.

The Notch lived up to its reputation. It was a massive boulder scramble, house-sized rocks scattered in a long maze with sheer stone walls closing in. Sometimes I had to crawl under, my pack scraping. In the shadows of those caves, ice still lingered in mid-June. Once, I had to push-pull my pack through a crack barely wide enough for my body. Another time, I braced my head against a rock just to keep from slipping as I searched for a foothold.

By the time we reached Mahoosuc Arm, I was already wrung out. The Arm was worse, a brutal climb straight up a 3,700-foot stone face. Poles were useless; I clawed upward with hands and feet. Thank God the weather was dry. I couldn't imagine doing it wet. Stopping wasn't an option; lose momentum and you risked sliding right off. I honestly don't know how SOBOs made it down.

At the top of Speck Mountain, I stopped to catch my breath and called Stephanie. Black flies swarmed me, but I needed to hear her voice. "This isn't hiking," I told her. "This is rock scrambling."

Sundance was so drained that he actually napped at the top of the Arm. I reached Speck Pond Campsite by 4:00 p.m.; he stumbled in an hour later. A NOBO named Scrambles joined us briefly before heading on. Two others, Pre and One Stick, showed up later. They had hiked the AT in 1998 and were back for a five-day adventure—though I couldn't imagine why anyone would choose this stretch again. To me, it felt more like punishment than adventure.

That day was a new low in pace: nine hours for just five miles. My body was battered, my spirit worn, but at least I was still moving.

June 18, 2016 – Saturday

I left camp at 7:00 a.m., with Sundance still packing up. He waved me on, and I promised to wait for him at Grafton Notch State Park, our agreed lunch spot. The climb up Old Speck Mountain didn't feel so bad. After wrestling with the Mahoosuc Notch and the Arm, these vertical climbs almost felt manageable. Maybe I was getting used to the terrain, or maybe my mood was simply better.

I laughed, remembering how, back in Georgia, I thought the early climbs were tough. Compared to this, those first miles seemed like child's play.

I reached Grafton Notch and waited an hour before deciding to push on to Baldpate Lean-to. Other hikers told me Sundance was on his way, so I trusted he'd catch up. Again, the climb wasn't as bad as I'd anticipated. Still, I lingered at the Lean-to, hoping he'd show. Instead, I met three weekend hikers—old friends from Louisiana who had scattered to Maine and Texas but reunited on the trail. They were SOBOs and warned me the trail ahead was brutal. By nightfall, Sundance still hadn't arrived. I set up my tent, ate dinner, and tried not to worry. This wasn't the first time he'd changed plans without warning. Just as I was settling in for sleep, a new face appeared: a shaggy, gray-bearded hiker named Stumble Dwarf. He looked like he had walked straight out of a Tolkien film. You meet all kinds of people on the AT.

June 19, 2016 – Sunday

I left early, climbing Baldpate's West Peak by 6:40 a.m. The SOBOs had warned me it was rough, but I thought they oversold it. East Peak was beautiful—a vast stretch of walkable bedrock above the treeline. At the summit, I managed to catch a cell signal and called Stephanie. I admitted I was worried about Sundance, not having seen him since Friday. That's when I learned he was behind me all along. Without a cell signal, he'd asked a Grafton Park employee to phone his wife Jane, who then called Stephanie, at midnight, no less, to let her know I shouldn't worry. When Stephanie told me this, I felt such a rush of relief and gratitude that it brought tears to my eyes. How lucky I was to have her.

Buoyed by that connection, I began my descent. At first, it was walkable stone, but soon ladders and butt-slides became necessary. At one point, I stopped for water and realized with horror that my tent was gone. It must have slipped loose during one of those slides. I dropped my pack and backtracked half a mile, scanning every inch of trail, but there was no sign of it. Dejected, I returned to my pack, where I ran into a SOBO named Old School. He kindly offered to keep an eye out for my tent and pass it along to Sundance if he found it.

I pushed on to Frye Notch Lean-to and waited. Another SOBO, Flash, stopped by, and I asked him as well to watch for my missing tent. Flash brightened my mood with news about the NBA Finals Game 7 playing that very night, and as a Cleveland fan, he was buzzing with hope. Later, a NOBO named Sixty Also arrived, soon joined by his buddy Sixty, which was when I got the joke about their names.

I went back up the trail to scout for Sundance and was relieved to see him just ten minutes away. Even better, he had my tent! Once again, the trail community had come through. Hikers really did take care of one another.

By then, I had logged only 3.5 official miles, but with all the backtracking and climbing, it felt like double. Sundance looked beat from making up for his short day, but at least the weather had been kind. We agreed we'd probably need a Zero soon to recover.

June 20, 2016 – Monday

I was up and hiking by 6:30 a.m., starting with Surplus Mountain before descending steadily toward East B Hill Road and the shuttle stop for Andover. Along the way, I discovered some trail magic: beer and soda cooling in a stream. I lingered there with another hiker, Still Thomas, a young man with pine tree tattoos who had worked in engineering for the service and was heading to the University of Tennessee in the fall.

Unfortunately, a group of SOBOs showed up and ruined the moment. They guzzled every can, ignoring the unspoken rule of leaving some for others. Then they started smashing cans and whooping like they were at a frat party. Their behavior left a sour taste; it clashed with the civility I'd come to expect from hikers.

When Sundance caught up, we called for a shuttle to Pine Ellis Hiker Lodge, run by two older women, Naomi and Irene. There we cleaned up, bunked down, and shared the space with Shelob and a new hiker, Rusty. We walked into town for dinner at Mill Street Market, returned with Gatorade, and found more hikers had arrived, including Rerun and his daughter Bear. Sundance wasn't doing well. He had made the mistake of drinking wine instead of water on the trail, and dehydration caught up with him. He ended up phoning a doctor, who advised him to take time off. A Zero day was in order.

June 21, 2016 – Tuesday (Zero)

We treated ourselves to breakfast at the Red Hen, an excellent choice. Afterward, Sundance went off on his own while I stayed behind, swapping stories with two section hikers around my age, BeeBee and Slow. Later, I finished a novel I'd started the night before and made a couple of calls, left a message for Plus-Two, and spoke with Heather, the daughter of a work acquaintance who lived nearby. She had offered to help me when I got close, and it was comforting to know I had that support.

By midday, I was hungry and wandered to the General Store. At the snack bar, I met a family from Davidson, NC—Greg, Katherine, and their two kids—section hiking together for the summer. Greg, an Episcopal priest, invited me to sit with them. I teased the kids by inventing trail names for each of them. To my surprise, they decided to keep those names!

Later, Plus-Two returned my call, saying he might be able to join me around the Fourth of July. That lifted my spirits. I also chatted with Irene's son, who crafted jewelry out of shellacked moose droppings. Not exactly Tiffany's material, but certainly memorable. While I hadn't seen any moose yet, the droppings were plentiful enough to supply his business.

June 22, 2016 – Wednesday

We had breakfast at 6:00 a.m. and arranged a shuttle to South Arm Road, so we could slack-pack SOBO ten miles back to East B Hill Road. It was nearly 10:30 a.m. before we got on the trail, late by my standards.

The morning brought more of Maine's familiar rollercoaster terrain. By lunch, I reached Hall Mountain Lean-to just as a storm rolled in. I huddled there for 40 minutes, clothes growing clammy and cold, waiting for Sundance. When he arrived, we pressed on together. Thankfully, the rain eased, and the last six miles through a quiet pine forest lifted my spirits. The trail was littered with bear scat, but no bears in sight, a reminder of that old joke about what bears really do in the woods.

Hiking SOBO with light packs made the day easier; I couldn't imagine tackling those miles northbound with a full load. We finished at the road and waited for Gloria, our shuttle driver. Back at the Lodge, the place was packed with new hikers, good thing we had booked our bunks in advance. Shelob was there again, too, and I found myself smiling at her Tolkien-inspired trail name. Sometimes I thought of the AT as my own kind of quest, casting people I met as characters in a story.

June 23, 2016 – Thursday

The shuttle wasn't running until 9:00 a.m., so I spent the morning chatting with Naomi over coffee and a muffin. She shared pieces of her life story, tough years, illness, heartbreak, but what struck me most was her kindness. She had chosen to pour her energy into caring for hikers, and it showed.

When Gloria arrived, Sundance and I threw our packs in and headed back to the trail. By 9:20 a.m., we were climbing Old Blue Mountain. It took me two and a half hours to reach the summit, only to find the view a letdown. At least the climb wasn't as rough as SOBOs had made it sound. Experience had taught me to take their warnings with a grain of salt; new hikers often judged difficulty differently than I did.

With Sundance feeling better, we pushed on past our original plan. The trail had some rebar railings, but no treacherous ladders, and the boggy stretches were manageable on puncheons. We topped Elephant Mountain and pressed on to Bemis, ending the day at Bemis Mountain Lean-to.

I texted Plus-Two, Heather, and Stephanie to update them, grateful for the rare signal. I told Stephanie I hoped to reach Route 4 in Rangeley by Saturday. A brief rain shower flared my knee pain, but ibuprofen worked its magic. At only 8.7 miles, the day was short but merciful, and I was grateful for that as I drifted to sleep before hiker midnight.

June 24, 2016 – Friday

I was out of camp by 6:30 a.m., enjoying the early solitude. Morning dew, spider webs, and all, I cherished being first on the trail, watching the forest wake up.

On the first peak, I had enough signal to call Heather and confirm our plan to meet at Route 4 the next day, around noon. She had been following my journey through Stephanie's updates for years and was enthusiastic about finally meeting me. Her mother, Debbie, my former co-worker, had even offered me her trailer nearby for a place to rest when I reached that point.

The hike itself wasn't too difficult. The toughest part was a steep descent from Bemis Ridge down to Bemis Stream, which pounded my knees. But when I waded into the cold water, it felt heavenly on my aching feet. Crossing Route 17, I paused to take in a stunning view before climbing back into the woods. Ponds and ledges lined the way until I reached Sabbath Day Pond Lean-to by 12:45 p.m.

I wanted to push further, but when Sundance arrived, he was wiped out, so we stopped. That left us a nine-mile hike to meet Heather the next day. My knees ached enough that I admitted the shorter day was probably wise. As dusk fell, I sat listening to the haunting call of a loon across the pond. The sound echoed through the twilight, wild and beautiful. In that moment, sore and tired as I was, I felt at peace.

June 25, 2016 – Saturday

Sundance and I were up early, on the trail by 5:15 a.m. We'd both slept in the Lean-to to avoid the extra hassle of breaking down tents, and it paid off—we moved quickly. The walk to the road was mostly downhill, the easiest trail I'd seen in Maine so far. At Little Swiftwater Pond, I stopped for breakfast, making my oatmeal on the shore. It was one of the prettiest ponds I'd ever seen, like a picture postcard, green forest all around, with canoes pulled up on one side. I lingered, soaking it in.

We reached the highway well before noon and waited for Heather, who pulled in at 12:30 p.m. The 90-minute ride to her place felt luxurious compared to hiking. She dropped us at her mother's trailer, where we showered and did laundry, then later invited us up to her house for dinner.

That evening, we met her husband, Jason, and their two boys, Everett (11) and Wyatt (8). They had been following my hike through Stephanie's emails, and Heather had even used stories from the trail as geography and history lessons for the kids. Everett and Wyatt were bursting with excitement to meet me, and I loved talking with them about the hike and their own interests. Heather cooked a feast: roast pork, macaroni and cheese, salads, and more, and we ate like kings. We stayed late, enjoying the company of such a warm family, before heading back to the trailer to sleep.

June 26, 2016 – Sunday (Zero)

We decided on a Zero. I watched a movie on TV, and Heather drove us to a nearby store for supplies, including a new battery for my watch. That evening, we were invited back to the family home for another meal. Everett and I talked soccer, while Wyatt proudly showed me a cookbook he had created. Jason offered to give us a ride back to the trail in the morning before work, which meant another early start.

As I lay down that night, I reflected on the kindness of this family. They didn't know us at all, yet they went out of their way to make us feel at home. Years later, I'd still be in touch with them. That's the magic of the trail, it brings people together in ways you don't forget.

June 27, 2016 – Monday

Jason dropped us back at the trail by 6:50 a.m., and we started up Saddleback Mountain. It was tough, but not quite the monster I had feared from other hikers' reports. Or maybe we were finally in better shape than we gave ourselves credit for. Still, with three peaks in the range, each over 4,000 feet, "not too bad" was all relative.

I reached Poplar Ridge Lean-to by 3:30 p.m., and Sundance rolled in about a half-hour later. Hiking 10.7 miles felt like a victory in this terrain. The Lean-to was overflowing with nine summer camp kids, a handful of SOBOs, and even a dog, so we pitched our tents. I chatted a bit with two SOBOs, Speedo and Availability, before turning in.

June 28, 2016 – Tuesday

With rain forecast, we hit the trail by 5:30 a.m. After two long downhill hours, I reached the ford at Orbeton Stream. That place carried a shadow; I knew it was the last known location of a hiker whose body had only recently been found years after she went missing. She had wandered uphill instead of following the water down, camped hidden, and eventually died. Standing there in the thick forest, with rocks and undergrowth pressing in, I could see how it might happen. The thought chilled me.

Crossing the creek, I started up Lone Mountain, only to find my energy drained. The day before, I had felt strong, but then again, that had been after two nights of real food. Trail meals couldn't compete. Still, I reached Spaulding Mountain Lean-to by 11:20 a.m., covering eight miles in about six hours. Not bad for weary legs. Sundance arrived half an hour later. With the rain setting in, we stayed put. By evening, the Lean-to was packed with other hikers riding out the storm. Most were SOBOs; the NOBO bubble hadn't reached Maine yet.

June 29, 2016 – Wednesday

I left in the rain at 6:30 a.m., ahead of Sundance. Spaulding Mountain came first, then a ridge toward Sugarloaf. Along the way, I met an ornithologist who explained that two nearly identical thrushes lived up here, distinguishable only by their songs. He played both calls for me, and sure enough, as I crested the ridge, I spotted thrushes flitting through the low brush. Hearing both songs, I happily added them to my life list.

After ridge walking, the trail dropped steeply to the South Carrabassett River. I worried about the ford after all the rain, but the water was low enough to cross safely. Then came the twin Crocker peaks. On the way, I met three memorable hikers: Box, a friendly young SOBO; Ghostwalker, another SOBO who had battled Lyme disease; and Swiss Miss, a NOBO from Switzerland who asked to take my picture, saying I looked "interesting." She and I leapfrogged each other much of the day.

By late afternoon, the rain came hard again. When I finally staggered onto Route 27 near Stratton, I was soaked through—boots squelching, pack cover defeated, sleeping bag drenched. Even my watch gave out. I called for a shuttle to the Stratton Motel and scratched a giant note in the dirt for Sundance, hoping it wouldn't wash away.

By evening, I was clean, dry, and relieved. Sundance showed up later, along with Swiss Miss. I walked slowly to the laundromat, called Stephanie with an update, and then crashed hard, exhaustion finally catching up.

June 30, 2016 – Thursday

Sundance's ankle was bothering him, so he stayed behind for a Zero. I was restless. We talked it over and agreed to hike separately from now on. We had rarely walked together anyway, more like keeping the same evening destinations.

Still, losing even that loose companionship hit me harder than I expected. So much so that I left my water bottles behind at the hostel, a mistake I never made. Distracted, I had to wait for the shuttle driver to bring them on the next run. By 7:30 a.m. I was back on the trail.

I set an ambitious 15-mile goal, but the Bigelows humbled me. Four massive peaks over 4,000 feet drained every ounce of energy I had. The views, though, were spectacular. One side opened onto Flagstaff Lake, a man-made stretch created by damming. The other side showed ski slopes and a winding road, like I was looking down from an airplane. Far below, I could even see the summer camp the girls had come from, their trail intersecting the AT.

By evening, I was exhausted and stopped at Safford Notch Campsite. Sidewind, a SOBO, was already there, and later two more hikers rolled in, including Swiss Miss. Loneliness gnawed at me, but I found cell service and called Stephanie. Hearing her voice steadied me yet again.

July 1, 2016 – Friday

I climbed Little Bigelow early, and at the top, I decided to honor Naked Hiker Day—late, since this unofficial custom typically was on the summer solstice. I stripped down and hiked for about 20 minutes, laughing to myself until I heard voices on the trail. I dressed quickly, but it gave me a silly sort of satisfaction to have done it.

Later, I ran into Swiss Miss again, and this time I took *her* picture. My AT journey was winding toward its end, and I felt the urge to capture more memories before it was all over. For years, this hike had been an impossible dream. Now the finish line was within reach, and that thought felt surreal.

I lost the trail at Flagstaff Lake when a maze of white-blazed side trails confused me. My maps didn't show them, so I had to backtrack to rejoin the AT. With the detour, I only made it as far as West Carry Pond Lean-to. A few SOBOs, Bigface and Badfoot, were there, along with the group of summer camp girls again. They played games noisily around the shelter, so I slipped down to the pond to soak my feet and enjoy some peace. By nightfall, I gratefully put in earplugs and drifted off.

July 2, 2016 – Saturday

My watch was still dead, so I hiked by sun and instinct, without my usual habit of tracking pace. It left me restless—numbers had been my way of marking progress, pushing forward. Still, I reached Pierce Pond Lean-to before midday. That surprised me; I was moving faster than I thought.

I had extra food, so I cooked ramen and tuna for lunch, a rarity, since I usually just nibbled on trail mix or crackers. A SOBO shared ginger snap cookies with me, making it a feast compared to my usual midday fare.

I would have pushed on, but the Kennebec River lay ahead, and the ferry didn't run in the afternoon. So I stayed at the lean-to for the night. I'd heard of Tim Harrison's camp and legendary pancakes nearby, and decided to make it a morning destination. That afternoon, the summer camp girls showed up again, along with three NOBOs—Tomahawk, Bumblebee, and Tigger. We agreed to go to Harrison's together for breakfast. I wandered Pierce Pond in the fading light, admiring its beauty. The night was cold, but perfectly clear.

July 3, 2016 – Sunday

We made our way to Harrison's camp for breakfast, and it lived up to its reputation. Pancakes the size of the plate, stuffed with fruit, plus juice and coffee—all for twelve bucks. The rustic fishing lodge leaned on uneven timbers, with a pool table propped six inches on one end, but the food was heavenly. I left happy and full, ready for the ferry.

At the Kennebec crossing, I was amazed to see Plus-Two waiting on the far bank! Stephanie had secretly coordinated the surprise with him. After the crossing, Plus-Two drove me and Tigger to the Sterling Inn in Caratunk, where I cleaned up. Then he whisked me into town for lunch. On the way, I picked up a new watch at the general store.

We talked and laughed, catching up like no time had passed. Before dropping me back at the Inn, Plus-Two floated the idea of joining me for a stretch near Monson if timing worked out. The thought lifted me.

That evening, I called Stephanie, overflowing with gratitude for her role in arranging the surprise. We talked for half an hour; a luxury compared to our usual rushed calls. Later, I napped, read a book from the Inn, chatted with the gregarious owner, and enjoyed a hearty dinner. By bedtime, I felt full, happy, and deeply content. It had been a wonderful day.

July 4, 2016 – Monday

Monday morning, I grabbed breakfast, caught the shuttle, and was back on the trail by 7:20 a.m., just like any other morning. The miles rolled by smoothly, about 15 in all, over Pleasant Pond Mountain and past Moxie Pond. With cabins dotting the shoreline, there were more people out than usual, families enjoying the holiday. My only real break in the solitude came when I caught a cell signal on top of the mountain and called Stephanie. Otherwise, the day felt uneventful.

By 4:00 p.m. I reached Bald Mountain Brook Lean-to. Just before it, I passed a summer camp girls' group setting up along the trail. The shelter itself filled quickly with SOBOs, including a couple from Switzerland. I ended up chatting with Giggles, an enthusiastic college student I'd met earlier at the Sterling Inn, and Tigger, another college student I'd crossed paths with a few days before. We all swapped trail stories while cooking dinner, and I found myself enjoying the company more than I expected. By 8:00 p.m. I was in my bag, drifting toward sleep. I didn't even realize until then that it had been the Fourth of July. Out here, it was just another day of walking.

July 5, 2016 – Tuesday

I hit the trail by 6:20 a.m. and made quick work of Moxie Bald Mountain. At the West Piscataquis River, I stripped down and waded across, letting the cold water double as both a bath and a relief for sore muscles. Afterward, though, the trail turned into a strange rollercoaster, up and down the riverbank for no obvious reason. I half-joked to myself that the trail planner must have been drunk that day.

I pushed hard, hoping to beat the summer camp girls to Horseshoe Canyon Lean-to and snag a tent site. But they'd gotten up for the sunrise on Moxie Bald and were already there when I arrived. A boys' group had shown up too, so every site was taken. Another night in the lean-to for me.

Around 3:00 p.m., when the campers disappeared into their tents, I wandered down to the river and found a secluded spot. I stripped again and stretched out in the current, letting the cool water wash away the sweat and soothe my aching knees. It was like slipping into a natural whirlpool. I sat on a sun-warmed rock to dry, grateful for the private moment.

Back at the shelter, Giggles, Tigger, and a mix of SOBOs and NOBOs filled the space. Salty, Waffle, Knarf, and Scenario, whom I'd met at Pine Ellis, were among them. The evening was typical trail chatter: gear, weather, and trail conditions. Some SOBOs slipped out with a flimsy excuse, and sure enough, the faint smell of pot drifted back. By 8:30 p.m., though, everyone had settled down. Another crowded, noisy night, but still part of the rhythm of the AT.

July 6, 2016 – Wednesday

I got up at 5:00 a.m., determined to stay ahead of the summer camp chaos, and was moving by 5:30 a.m. Tigger joined me, setting a brisk pace. Crossing the East Piscataquis River, I rock-hopped across, then stopped to cook breakfast on the far bank. Knarf, another older hiker, came by, and we shared a quiet moment before the peace was shattered by the arrival of the camp boys. I packed up and moved on quickly.

At Hebron Lake, I paused to take photos, and both Scenario and Knarf caught up. We chatted a bit before I pressed ahead through shady woods that took the edge off the summer heat. At my next break, Scenario offered me a ride into Monson, the final trail town for NOBOs, and I accepted.

In Monson, I checked into The Lakeshore House, finding myself the only hiker there. Most of the crowd had gone to Shaw's, the more raucous hostel down the road. I cleaned up, ate downstairs at the Pub, and met Carrie, the summer caretaker. Later, I watched an action movie on TV before heading to bed. Monson felt quiet, almost like the calm before a storm.

July 7, 2016 – Thursday (Zero)

I had planned a Zero in Monson to prepare for the last 114 miles, the Hundred-Mile Wilderness, and, at the end, Katahdin. I'd heard the Wilderness was tough and demanded enough food for up to 10 days, so careful planning was essential. After breakfast at Pete's Bakery, I collected the supply box I'd mailed ahead and spent the morning organizing gear.

With that chore done, I let myself relax. I flipped through TV channels, then picked up a book I found lying around: *The Laughalachian Trail* by Ledge. It was a humorous take on thru-hiking, and even mentioned Rebecka, the Lakeshore House owner. She herself was warm and kind, and I enjoyed chatting with her. When another hiker came in with an injured arm, Rebecka immediately arranged a ride to Greenville, the nearest town with medical care.

Later, Sundance appeared. Our paces had brought us back together after all, but his niece was coming to pick him up for a family vacation, so we wouldn't head into the Wilderness together. That evening, after a walk around the tiny town, I called Stephanie from the house phone. "I'm on the final stretch," I told her. Saying the words felt surreal. I ended the day with a Cobb salad from the Pub, my pack waiting by the bed. Tomorrow, it would be me versus the Wilderness.

July 8, 2016 – Friday

Sundance and I had one last breakfast together at Pete's before parting ways. Carrie gave me a ride back to the trailhead, and I was hiking by 7:30 a.m. The flat, wooded trail felt like a gift. I was moving well, proud, and almost giddy that I'd come so far.

Then, about four miles in, it all changed. Approaching North Pond, I slipped on a mossy rock and went down hard. My left knee twisted underneath me, my heel slamming into my butt under the full weight of my pack. The pain was sharp, but I got up and hobbled on, convinced I could walk it off.

Two miles later, at Little Wilson Falls, I stopped to swallow aspirin and pull a compression sleeve over my knee. But when I stood, the pain was worse. I tried again to shake it off, but by then I was limping badly. Day hikers noticed and offered help, pointing me to a side trail that led to a parking lot. If I could make it a mile, they'd drive me back to Monson. That limp was one of the longest miles of my life.

Back at the Lakeshore House, Rebecka stepped in once again, arranging an appointment with a doctor in Greenville. While I waited, I called Stephanie to tell her what had happened.

The doctor confirmed I'd torqued the knee badly. No ligament tears, but he ordered two to three weeks of rest before I could even *think* about hiking again.

Stephanie, though, had known before I did. She'd heard the dread in my voice when I'd called after the fall and had packed a bag, arranged weekend work coverage, and started driving east. By the time I called her in despair, she was already a few hours down the road. God, I love that woman.

I tried to pass the time with Sleepyhead, a fellow section hiker sharing my bunkroom. We talked a lot, and I found myself wishing he'd been my hiking partner. Two others arrived, Bell, who reminded me of a young Stephanie, and Jack. We watched TV, shared a sandwich from the Pub, and tried to keep spirits light. But when I went to bed, the weight of failure pressed harder than the pain in my knee.

July 9, 2016 – Saturday (off the trail)

Sleep was scarce, and the pain, frustration, and self-anger kept me tossing. Why now? Why here, so close? I awoke depressed and angry at the unfairness of falling so close to the end.

By morning, I was too restless to sit still, but I couldn't even get up and down the stairs, so I relied on the kindness of others to shuttle food and drink to me up on the second-floor room.

Sleepyhead brought me a cinnamon bun from Pete's, and we all sat watching Serena Williams win Wimbledon. I kept glancing at the road, waiting for Stephanie.

She arrived around 5:00 p.m., after nearly 600 miles of driving. I should have been grateful just to see her, but I couldn't bear staying in that bunkhouse one more night. I insisted we leave immediately.

She wanted to rest, but I was done—done with Monson, done with limping, done with being surrounded by hikers moving forward when I couldn't.

I promised I could drive; it was my left knee, not my right. She wrestled my pack into the car, and after quick goodbyes to Sleepyhead and Rebecka, we pulled away. We only made it as far as Augusta before stopping. The thin motel walls gave us little rest, but I didn't care. I just wanted the distance between me and the dream slipping through my fingers.

Interlude: August 16, 2016 – Tuesday

Weeks later, the truth came clear. After some rest, I started biking, then walking the neighborhood. The pain flared again. An MRI showed a torn meniscus, a stress fracture, a Baker's cyst, and advanced arthritis. The orthopedic surgeon was stunned to hear I'd been hiking and intended to return to finish the AT. "Well, your knees are already shot," he said. "The AT can't make them worse."

The physician's assistant ordered six to eight weeks of no activity, then physical therapy. My 2016 hike was finished.

So close. So damn close.

Chapter 12

Completion

Maine

June 13, 2017 – Tuesday (Back to the AT)

Another year. Just over 100 miles to go, and you'd think I'd be jubilant, but I wasn't. Instead, I felt hollow and low. The stress fracture and knee injury from last season had haunted me all year, and though I'd worked hard at recovery, age was catching up with me. I'd be 66 in the fall. Arthritis gnawed at my knees, feet, and even the discs in my back.

The young physical therapist I'd seen did not seem to believe me when I said I planned to return to the AT. She treated me like an old man, giving me mild, gentle exercises instead of the hard training I knew I needed. My leg had healed, but my back still hurt. I feared what carrying a heavy pack would do to me. I had no confidence in my body—only my innate tenacity pulled me back to the AT. After everything I'd endured to get this far, I *had* to finish the whole trail.

I drove myself to Monson, Maine, over two days. With so little left, it made sense to leave my car parked there and get a ride back after I finished. Monson, the closest trail town to Baxter State Park, was a natural gathering point for northbound finishers. The Lakeshore House agreed to hold my car, since I'd be staying there.

I arrived earlier than expected, pleased, because I thought I could secure my Katahdin hiking permit there. But at the Monson ATC office, I discovered the rules had changed: permits were now issued only at Katahdin Stream Campground. That left me with the rest of the day unstructured. Had I known, I might have started hiking right away. Instead, I lingered at the inn.

A couple of SOBOs were starting their hikes, but they weren't very friendly. I picked up a humorous book, read for a while, and indulged in an afternoon nap. I made arrangements with Rebecka, the same friendly proprietor from last year, for a shuttle back to Little Wilson Falls the next morning, so I could skip the painful four-mile stretch I'd completed before having to limp off the AT. Later, two more SOBOs, Dot and Frankenfoot, arrived. They had met in Bangor and started hiking together from Katahdin. That evening, we watched a movie together, though I excused myself when they put on a second one that didn't suit me.

A combination of aches and pains joined my racing thoughts to keep me up. I had a terrible night's sleep. Not an auspicious start.

June 14, 2017 – Wednesday

I awoke at 6 a.m., my usual time, and walked next door to Pete's for a hearty breakfast. Buddy, the shuttle driver, arrived promptly at 6:45 a.m. for the quick ride to Little Wilson Falls. Buddy gave me his card in case I needed a ride anywhere along the trail. Although this stretch was called the "Hundred Mile Wilderness" because there were no towns or roads, Buddy explained that there were logging roads and he knew every one of them. If I needed help, I would have a ride out. I was grateful but hoped I wouldn't need the assistance. After a little good-natured ribbing about football (Buddy had the tragic flaw of being a fan of the Patriots, the arch rivals of my Buffalo Bills), we said goodbye, and I started what I hoped was my final section of the AT.

By 7:15 a.m. I was back on the trail. The weather was perfect, and my spirits lifted as I met SOBO hikers headed south: Packed Meat, Smokey and his dog Bandit (aka Ollie, yes, even the dog had a trail name), then later at Vaughn Stream I met Switchback and Voices. I loved those brief trail connections to get me in the hiker mentality before continuing north.

The trail was not as bad as I feared: small ups and downs, a track sometimes faint but always marked by the white blazes. Down south, with so many hikers, the path is worn smooth. Up here, you really rely on those blazes.

I had planned to push all the way to Cloud Pond, but by the time I began the ascent up Barren Mountain, exhaustion forced me to stop at Long Pond Stream Lean-to. Barely over eight miles. Not a good sign.

Two things worried me. First, my vision blurred when I grew tired, something entirely new. I had to stop and let my sight clear before searching out the next blaze.

Was I losing my vision? The thought scared me badly. Second, the lower back pain I'd feared started almost immediately. Months of physical therapy hadn't fixed it.

Fortunately, a break in the gloom came when I met Preacher and Stretch, a married couple heading south. Later, more SOBOs drifted in, pitching tents nearby. Their company lifted me, and I stayed put rather than forcing more miles. I swapped stories with the new hikers, telling them about what awaited as they moved south.

But when hiker midnight came, I crawled into my bag, anxious. My back still throbbed. My body felt wrecked, and this had been an easy day. Was I doomed to be unable to complete my goal after all of this time and effort?

June 15, 2017 – Thursday (off the trail again)

I woke at 5:30 a.m., restless and hurting. During the night, I had made a hard decision. Continuing into the mountains with a back that only got worse would be reckless. If it failed entirely, I'd be stuck.

I called Buddy. He directed me down to Long Pond Creek and walked in himself to meet me. From there, he led me along a bushwhacked path to reach a logging road where his car waited. By 9:00 a.m. I was back in Monson.

I grabbed a sandwich at Pete's, picked up my car keys from Carrie at Lakeshore House, and pointed my car toward Buffalo. I drove straight through, arriving late that night to Stephanie's startled surprise.

I was the most depressed she'd ever seen me. I felt like the last few days had been a total waste. I was furious: I'd done every bit of physical therapy, even trained with a pack, yet it hadn't helped. How could I collapse so fast? And the blurred vision terrified me. Stephanie suggested dehydration, but I doubted it. Still, as I ticked through the issues aloud, I realized I had been right to bail. If I'd stayed, I would have been crawling.

I told her I'd need to rebuild both physically and mentally before I could try again, if I ever could. Maybe this was the end.

Interlude – June-July 2017

Nathan, my son, convinced me to see his chiropractor friend, Patrick. I went reluctantly, but within a couple of weeks of adjustments and specific exercises, I felt better than I had after a year of PT.

My back pain receded. The blurry vision vanished without explanation. By the end of four weeks, I felt strong again, almost reborn.

I was deeply grateful to Patrick. And with my strength returning, I knew what I had to do. It was time to try again.

August 8, 2017 – Tuesday (and…back)

Unbelievable. I was headed back to the AT. I had left Buffalo the day before, taking an easy two-day drive this time. When I pulled into Monson that afternoon, I checked once again into the Lakeshore House. I texted Stephanie and Plus-Two to let them know I was safe.

I wandered over to Shaw's, the other hiker hostel in town, and arranged a shuttle with Poet to Otter Pond, near the spot I had left the trail in June. Back at the Lakeshore House, I swapped stories with a couple of hikers. Tom, a disillusioned section hiker, was calling it quits. Oh Man, a NOBO from Corning, NY, was still pushing north. We watched a movie together, then I picked up the same humorous book I'd abandoned two months earlier. It felt good to slip back into that rhythm. I went to bed at hiker midnight in much better spirits.

August 9, 2017 – Wednesday

I slept fairly well and decided to head over to Shaw's for breakfast. It was fantastic: $10 for endless pancakes, eggs, bacon, juice, and coffee. I sat at a big family-style table among hikers, swapping stories. I especially enjoyed talking with Pathfinder, a NOBO from Arkansas, about Razorback football. There was even a hiker from Portugal at the table.

AJ from Shaw's gave me a lift to Otter Pond. The access trail was well-marked, and soon I stood once more on the AT, exactly where I had left off. I turned north and began climbing Barren Mountain.

The terrain was typical of Maine: rocks, roots, and rugged climbs. I was tired and sore, but it was a different kind of soreness now: the good kind, the kind that comes from exercise. The terrifying back pain was gone. I slowed quickly, but I didn't mind. This time, I could stop and enjoy the breathtaking views. I didn't need to hurry.

By 6:00 p.m. I reached Chairback Gap Lean-to, a cramped shelter wedged onto a hillside. The space was packed, so I pitched my tent on the only marginally flat spot nearby, perched just above a drop-off to a stream. It barely fit, but it would do.

That night, I ate dinner with a dentist from Ohio and a hiker from the Czech Republic. I was relaxed and happy, and surprised myself with a rare good night's sleep.

August 10, 2017 – Thursday

Waking up rested was such a welcome change. I ate breakfast, packed up, and was on the trail by 6:15 a.m. As always, I liked to start the morning with a climb when I was fresh, but Chairback Mountain tired me out right away. The view at the top, though, made the effort worth it. Starting down was another story with a near vertical tumble of rocks forming what was called the "back" of the "chair." There wasn't really a defined trail, just a lot of rock hopping. On steep downhills, I always felt off balance, as if my pack might pitch me forward, but I made it down safely. The "seat" of the mountain was a roller coaster of rock and root, but at least the trip down went faster than I expected.

I looked for landmarks I had read about, but never saw them, so I was surprised when the trail spit me out at Katahdin Ironworks Road. After crossing, I had to ford Pleasant River, the cool water washing over my bare feet while I carried my hiking boots to keep them dry, which was a simple but welcome relief. Sitting on the far bank to pull my boots back on, I met a hiker named Tink. He had started the AT 25 years ago and was finally completing his last section northbound. I smiled to myself, maybe six years wasn't so bad after all.

The rest of my morning was a gradual incline past Gulf Hagas to Carl A. Newhall Lean-to. I arrived by 1:00 p.m., too beat to go further, so I decided to camp there. Renaissance Man, a 78-year-old section hiker from New Hampshire, was already there. He carried a ton of trail history in his head, and I was amazed at how well he was doing. Here I was in my mid-sixties, feeling like I was falling apart. Later, Portuguese, a travel writer from Lisbon, rolled in. He and I had crossed paths back at Shaw's. The three of us passed a warm, lighthearted afternoon talking and joking. Toward evening, a woman named F-Stop arrived with her dog Lief. Everyone was in bed early, by 8:00 p.m.

August 11, 2017 – Friday

I slipped out by 6:15 a.m., watching the clouds thicken. The threat of rain pushed me into a faster pace, and I made good time over West Peak and along Hay Mountain. But by the time I started climbing White Cap, the skies opened. At the summit, I paused, entranced, as clouds rose up out of the valley only to be torn apart by the wind.

I tried to capture it in a photo, but I knew the scene was too alive, too moving, to be trapped in a still frame.

On the way down, I was relieved to find stone stairs. Uneven, yes, but infinitely better than sliding across wet rock. I rated them the best-built steps I'd seen on the trail. By noon I reached Logan Stream Lean-to for lunch, where Portuguese caught up to me. After resting together, I pushed on toward East Branch Lean-to. It was all downhill, and to my delight, I clocked better than two miles per hour, even in the rain. Along the way, I spotted a Black & White Warbler and, to my surprise, a Spruce Grouse standing boldly by the trail, rare and seemingly waiting to be noticed.

I arrived at the shelter by 2:15 p.m. and stretched out until Portuguese came in. The rain had passed, so I strung out my damp gear to dry in the sun. It had been a short day of hiking, but I wasn't going to push hard and risk another injury. Later, Oh Man arrived, someone I had met back in Monson. He offered to meet me at Antlers Campsite the next night. Plow, another hiker, came by intending just to rest but decided to stay when the rain picked back up. That night, we had a merry little crew, laughter carrying into the woods until sleep called us all.

August 12, 2017 – Saturday

I got up and was out by 6:30 a.m., aiming to meet Oh Man at Antlers Campsite, a 16-mile day, double my recent distance. The skies stayed cloudy, cool, and good for hiking. I started slow with Little Boardman Mountain but soon settled into a rhythm, pleased to be holding two miles an hour. At Cooper Brook Falls Lean-to I rested briefly with Portuguese and a hiker named Pumba. The falls were beautiful, but I pushed on. The promise of meeting someone was a strong motivator.

At Jo-Mary Road, I realized I still had four miles to Antlers. My legs sagged, but Plow caught me, and we hiked near each other, chatting about his life. He held a high position at a software company but spent his free time winter hiking, bicycling, and even doing rescues. Smart, personable, and decades younger than me, he kept me moving when I might have slowed.

Reaching Antlers, Plow continued on, but I stopped. It was the most beautiful campsite I had seen on the trail. Nestled among pines, it sat right at the edge of Jo-Mary Lake, the wind murmuring softly through the trees. Portuguese stopped briefly before pressing on. Oh Man had moved on, too. I was alone.

I had a cell signal and called Stephanie. Her voice filled me with such comfort. As we talked, rain began, and I hurried to set up my tent. I tossed all my gear inside, even my clothes, then waded waist-deep into the lake. Washing the sweat and grime of days past felt incredible. I emerged, planning to air-dry naked, but when I heard voices, I dove back into my tent, laughing at myself as I scrambled into clothes. Moments later, Piper and Lulu Bell appeared. I confessed about my "bath," and they teased me about how narrowly they had missed a show. Later, I called Stephanie back, and we laughed together about my skinny-dipping misadventure. That evening, after dinner, I wandered the shoreline. The lake stretched quiet and endless, and I promised myself I'd return someday just to stand in that spot again.

August 13, 2017 – Sunday

I allowed myself a slow start, knowing it would be a short day. At the dock for White House Landing, Plow was already there, waiting. Bill, the owner, ferried us across in his boat to the off-the-grid lodge on Pemadumcook Lake.

There I showered, drank a root beer, and spent the afternoon happily chatting at picnic tables with other hikers. Purple Crayon was waiting for a seaplane after hiking with his son. Noon Noodle, a young woman from Connecticut, was flip-flopping. A couple from Vermont arrived with huge packs, each complete with a chair. They grinned and told me they liked to be comfortable. Secretly, I dubbed them "the furniture couple."

Later, I called Stephanie and learned Plus-Two couldn't meet me as we'd hoped because family responsibilities had him babysitting his grandson. I felt the pang of disappointment but understood. That evening, I sat with Hats, whose bad knees made mine look young, and Pathfinder, whom I had met in Monson. We ate homemade pizza and burgers, laughter mixing with anticipation. Mt. Katahdin wasn't visible yet, but we could all feel it nearby.

After dinner, I went into the bunkhouse and called Plus-Two. We made tentative plans to meet at Katahdin and summit together, if Plus-Two could get off work that Thursday, which was when I figured I would arrive at the base of the mountain. Settling into the bunk bed, I found it far more comfortable than a sleeping bag on a lean-to floor or tent, but it was still a restless night.

August 14, 2017 – Monday

Bill fixed us breakfast and boated us back to the trail. It started gentle but quickly turned rough as we climbed Nesuntabunt Mountain. The woods were shadowy, eerie, almost Tolkien-esque, like hobbits entering Mordor. At the summit, Katahdin stood alone on the horizon. My heart leapt. I took a picture, my first sight of the mountain I had chased for six years.

Plow and I leapfrogged much of the day. The descent was a mess, all rocks, roots, and boulders tossed together with no discernable path. By evening, I reached Rainbow Stream Lean-to and pitched my tent to escape the mosquitoes. Plow and I found a quiet swimming hole nearby and stripped down, diving in. Lying naked in the cool water, I let days of sweat and strain wash away. Back at camp, I ate packaged lasagna and lay awake, my mind buzzing with the nearness of my dream.

August 15, 2017 – Tuesday

I rose with the sun, restless with excitement, and was hiking by 6:30 a.m. Rainbow Lake was beautiful, though the trail around it was the usual Maine jumble of rock and root. By noon, I had 11½ miles behind me. In the afternoon, I fell in step with Plow and Pathfinder. Together, we decided to camp at Abol Bridge.

There, for the first time, Katahdin filled the sky. From our campsite, it loomed massive beyond the river. I bought an energy drink from the store, a small celebration, while Plow went tubing and Pathfinder napped. I did laundry, showered, and soaked in the comfort of simple luxuries. Rain came by 7:00 p.m., and noisy vacation campers filled the night, but I was grateful for earplugs. Tomorrow would bring me to the base of Katahdin.

August 16, 2017 – Wednesday

Pathfinder and I waited for the camp restaurant to open at 7:00 a.m., eager for hot food. After breakfast, we signed up for sites at the Birches Campsite, the base camp for Katahdin. I was hiker number five; Pathfinder, six.

We moved briskly that morning. At a ford, I slipped and soaked my boots, but laughed at the cold water against my feet. At another crossing, Pathfinder stumbled and gashed his cheek, but he was alright. Nothing could stop us now that we were so close. By afternoon, we signed in at Katahdin Stream and hiked on to the Birches.

The tent sites were poor, so I chose the lean-to. I lay down briefly but woke when Ranger Justine came by to register us and hand out our permits.

That night, a group of us gathered, NOBOs all, brimming with anticipation. For once, we shared our real names, our real stories, the reasons we were out here. It was the most personal, honest conversation I had on the trail. All of us realized that the end of the trek and return to "real" life was imminent.

August 17, 2017 – Thursday

I was restless with excitement and up and packed by 5:30 am. A rigidly prescribed number of hikers were allowed a permit each day, and they were required to summit and return to base camp the same day to be tracked. Mt. Katahdin could be dangerous, and hikers could go missing. No one was allowed to stay on the mountain overnight, so they had to leave their main packs at the ranger station and were loaned a daypack with water and essentials like a first aid kit to pack for the climb and return. I ate a bigger breakfast than usual to stoke up for the intense day.

Pathfinder was slow packing his daypack, and my nerves wouldn't let me stand around. I set out alone at 7:00 a.m. on the Hunt Trail, buzzing with anticipation. The first couple of miles were steady uphill, not as tough as I had feared. But then I crossed the tree line, and everything changed. The wind roared at forty miles an hour, icy gusts cutting through me. Clouds whipped past at eye level, as though I had walked into another world. For a moment, I thought of the *Lord of the Rings* again, because it felt that strange and otherworldly.

At one point, I met a woman who was already turning back. She couldn't stay upright in the fierce wind. For a split second, I wondered if I should do the same. But I had come too far. I tucked away my hiking sticks and scrambled on all fours, clinging to rock and rebar at the infamous "Monkey Bars" section. I learned later that several hikers turned back right there. But I couldn't. I wasn't going to quit now. Not after six years, not after two thousand miles.

Finally, I pulled myself onto the Flatlands; a mile and a half of rocky but level ground. Relief washed over me, though the wind still howled. And then, ahead, I saw them: Ghetto, Low-Tech, and Hickory, the NOBOs I'd chatted with last night, waiting at the summit. The moment was surreal. We hugged, fist-bumped, maybe even cried a little. Hickory snapped my picture at the iconic wooden sign. There it was, the proof.

I had walked from Springer Mountain in Georgia to the top of Katahdin in Maine. Six years, more than two thousand miles, and a lifetime of memories all ending here on this peak.

The view was stunning, though oddly familiar, like echoes of other peaks I'd climbed on the AT. Strangely, it didn't hit me right away. The enormity of what I'd done hadn't sunk in yet. I sat for a while, snapping pictures, waiting for Pathfinder. After thirty minutes, the cold drove me down the trail. I met him on his way up and wished him well, proud that he, too would soon claim this finish.

On the descent, I took the side trail to Abol Campsite, as the rangers had suggested. It was shorter, steeper, and brutal on the knees, at times I had to scoot down on my backside, at others, I climbed carefully down sheer rocks. Finally, switchbacks appeared and made things easier. Low-Tech and Sally later spotted me walking the road and gave me a ride back to my pack, then into Millinocket.

That night, at the Pamola Motor Lodge, I celebrated with Hickory, Low-Tech, and Pathfinder when he arrived. Over beers and dinner, we toasted to our shared victory. Tomorrow, I would arrange my ride back to Monson, and be on my way home, to my beautiful wife, to my wonderful family.

August 18, 2017 – Friday (home again)

I woke at my usual 6:00 a.m., had breakfast with Low-Tech, Sally, and Hickory, and said my goodbyes. Buddy picked me up and got me back to Monson by 11:30 a.m. After a quick lunch, I grabbed my car and pointed it toward Buffalo. Twelve and a half hours of rain and traffic couldn't dim my spirit. Nothing could. I was going home.

I pulled in just after midnight. Stephanie met me at the garage door. I dropped my pack, pulled her into my arms, and kissed her. We held on tight, neither of us speaking, just clinging as though we could make up for every mile of separation in that one embrace.

From my last journal entry – August 20, 2017

Well, this adventure is complete. It will never be finished because it will always be replayed in my mind and heart. What did I get from the AT?

I learned I am stronger than I think I am. We are surrounded by many things that make our lives complicated. The AT teaches simplicity. The trail is unforgiving, especially in Maine. Maine is Mean has a lot of resonance in my thoughts. Maine is also beautiful. I learned that there are many wonderful people out there on the AT.

146

When you get to know them, you will realize that they are wonderful off the AT. It renews my faith in Humanity. Nature and God's creations are essential to remaining grounded in the world and in life. I love my family. Loneliness can be very powerful in determining a successful hike. I will probably miss being out there, but not the pain of hiking.

Maine is beautiful. The whole Trail is beautiful. Nature is wonderful. I complained about the trail condition, but it is a treasure of the country that is underappreciated. When I started, I met someone who did it 13 times. I never understood even doing it a second time. But after I finished, there were so many things I would want to do differently and re-hike. Probably twice as many things I didn't see or do along the way. Learned as I went to appreciate it more and more. But I wish they would mark it better.

I complained a lot - that was my impetus, I wouldn't let it beat me. If I kept it in, I might have been down on the trail. Would have lost interest. Needed the fight -- complain, and get it out there and beat it. Motivate. I did the workers an injustice by complaining; they do work hard, but can't do everything.

What next? Learn to play the flute :) Or make flutes instead, play the recorder. No plan for what is next. I just finished AT, have a beautiful wife and lovely children and grandchildren, what more do I need?

The End

Acknowledgments

This book would not have been written if it wasn't for my wife and coauthor, Stephanie. She first encouraged me to believe it was possible, showed me what I needed to do and then supported me throughout the journey. Later, she got me to sit down and talk about my hike, capturing the story in my words. She also found us a wonderful editor, Katrina Nichols, to help refine those words into a great story. Stephanie is a treasure that inspires me and many others to follow their dreams. Got to love that woman!

My children also gave me support and love the whole time I hiked. At times they probably thought I was crazy, and they may be right.

A special thanks to all the hikers I encountered along the way, especially Plus-Two, Sundance, Blue, Mouse and Steve-O. I am also grateful to my nephew Mike who started out with me, and to my sister Pam and her husband Les for the time spent schlepping me around and feeding me. And of course, thanks to all the Trail Angels supplying Trail Magic that I happened upon over those years.

Finally, I am deeply grateful to the Appalachian Trail Conservancy (ATC) for their dedication in planning and maintaining this incredible trail. Their tireless work—and that of their partners—makes journeys like mine possible. I encourage anyone inspired by this story to consider supporting the ATC so the Appalachian Trail can continue to be experienced for generations to come.

www.ingramcontent.com/pod-product-compliance
Lightning Source LLC
Chambersburg PA
CBHW071014200326
41589CB00001B/1